how to smell like God

true stories burning with the scent of heaven

how to smell like God

true stories burning with the scent of heaven

steven james

refuge™

an imprint of
Standard Publishing
www.rfgbooks.com

dedication

To M.C., a man who has smelled like God as long as I've known him.

acknowledgments

Portions of the story about Crystal Sturgill in chapter five first appeared in the May/June 2000 issue of *Campus Life* magazine. My thanks goes out to Crystal for letting me share her story, and to *With*, *Campus Life*, *Breakaway*, *Real Time*, *Zelos*, *Conqueror*, *Encounter*, *YouthWalk*, *Devo'zine* and *Insight* magazines for publishing various stories included in this book.

special thanks

To my friend, Eddie Brittain, for his insights and honesty; to my editor, Dale Reeves, for his encouragement and passion for youth; to my pastor, Tom Oyler, for teaching the truths that have echoed through my mind and found their way onto these pages; and to my wife, Liesl, for always honoring me and loving my daughters.

| 12 | 11 | 10 | 09 | 08 | 07 | 06 | 05 |
| 5 | 4 | 3 | 2 | 1 | | | |

ISBN: 0-7847-1775-3

Project editors: Dale Reeves and Greg Holder
Cover photo © Sparky/Getty Images/The Image Bank
Cover and inside design by Ahaa! Design/Dina Sorn
Copyediting: Patricia Senseman

contents

what's that smell?

When I first met Tanya, I knew she was different. Part of it was the way she acted. The way she smiled. The way she looked at you. She wasn't like most 17-year-old girls you meet. How can I say this . . . she *smelled* different from other people.

Not physically, it was more like the aroma of her whole life.

Then, when I met Seth, I smelled the same thing. And Josh and Brook and Chris all smelled that way, too.

What is that smell?

Over the years, I've met hundreds of teenagers who all smell the same.

Then, one day when I was reading 2 Corinthians 2:14-16, I realized what they smelled like.

Those students smelled like God.

The fragrance of their lives was different from the stench of the world. You could tell when you were with them. Their attitudes and priorities and lifestyles were *different*. They smelled like they didn't belong on this planet, like they were made for a better place. It was the fragrance of heaven. Strong. Powerful. Life-changing.

And the amazing thing is, you can smell just like them. You can smell like God, too.

Look at what the apostle Paul writes,

"Now wherever we go he [God] uses us to tell others about the Lord and to spread the Good News like a sweet perfume. Our lives are a fragrance presented by Christ to God" (2 Corinthians 2:14, 15).

Another Bible translation puts it like this, "*For we are to God the aroma of Christ" (NIV)*. They're both saying the same thing: When you become a Christian you start to smell like God. The old nasty habits begin to fade. And other people can't help but notice the difference.

"Okay," you're probably saying, "So what does that mean, anyhow—smelling like God? What in the world does God smell like? And how exactly do people spread the fragrance of Christ? What does *that* mean?"

Well, that's what this book is all about, going from body odor to godly odor. From the smell of earth to the fragrance of heaven.

In the pages of this book you'll meet real people like Matt*, a rock climber who fell 85 feet and got a second chance at life; Crystal, a 19-year-old convicted mass murderer who found hope behind bars; Dan, a high school wrestler from Illinois who went to the mat with a deadly snake; Joe, a college freshman who called his room the "porno pit"; Maria, a cute college sophomore who asked me a question that changed the course of my life; and me, a normal guy who struggled and wondered and questioned and finally found what he was looking for.

Some of the people you'll meet smelled like God, some didn't. But through their stories—and mine—you'll see God's story played out. And, if you pay attention, you'll even catch a glimpse (or a whiff) of yourself.

Learning to smell like God is a journey that begins with faith as you realize who God is, and discover his amazing plan for your life.

So, if you're ready for the adventure . . . if you're ready to smell like Tanya, Seth, Josh, Brook and Chris . . . then turn the page and discover for yourself what it means to smell like God.

* The stories in this book are true. All the people you meet are real people. Some names, places, conversations and identities have been changed to protect the privacy of the people involved.

getting to know the Father

The worst thing I've ever smelled was Corey's feet.

We'd been hiking for a couple of weeks through a desert in southern Texas when he started to complain about sores on his feet. Then, so we could see if he had an infection, he took off his boots.

Yikes.

That boy needed some industrial-strength deodorizers!

Well, before we can approach God, we need some industrial strength deodorizers, too. Not in our *soles*, but in our *souls*.

We need some spiritual Odor-eaters. Because there are things in our lives (in our thoughts and in our hearts) that stink to God.

In this section, you'll discover seven truths about your relationship with God. Each truth will act like a spiritual deodorizer when you apply it to your life.

Before you can ever smell like God, you need to understand a little about God's character and how you measure up to his holy requirements. It's not an easy journey. It takes honesty and humility, but if you're ready, let's get started.

It's the first step to smelling less like Corey and more like God.

the day we let stumpy out of the locker

If God really exists, what difference does that make to me? How does that affect my life? Do I even matter to God?

It was easy to make fun of Mark—a head shorter than the rest of the kids in our class, tangled hair, acne covering his face . . . and the clothes he wore made him look like a walking rummage sale.

You know the kind of guy he was. When we were hanging around talking with our friends and he came walking down the hall, we kinda closed up the circle so he couldn't slip in and join our group. And when we were eating in the cafeteria and he sat down at our table, we'd all remember something "important" to do and get up—one by one—leaving him sitting there all alone.

You know the kind of guy he was.

No one called him by his real name. We just called him Stumpy.

At least that's what we called him to his face.

Stumpy didn't play any sports. He wasn't in drama or band or on the honor roll. He didn't go to football games. Stumpy managed to slip through all the cracks. He didn't fit into any clique. Stumpy's only companion was this tall lanky kid whom everyone called Goose.

They always hung out together. Goose had Stumpy sharpen his pencils, do his homework, and buy candy bars for him. In return, Goose spent time with Stumpy. But I guess I shouldn't be too hard on him, because that was more than anyone else at my high school was willing to do.

Stumpy and Goose spent long afternoons in a deserted corner of the Student Union playing cards during their lunch hour, free time, and after school.

For the first month of school I didn't pay much attention to them. But as I slid between the cliques myself, I began to spend more and more time learning to play poker with Goose and Stumpy, watching my afternoons slip away in the Student Union.

What I remember most about Stumpy was locking him in a locker.

"let me out!"

It just sorta happened one day. We were playing cards after school. Other than the three of us, the room was deserted. Suddenly, Goose winked at me and mouthed the words, "Follow my lead." I shrugged my shoulders and nodded.

Goose stood up. "Hey, Stumpy, could you help me get something out of my locker?"

"Sure, Goose, I guess. What do you need?"

"Just this," said Goose, grabbing Stumpy by one arm. I jumped up and caught hold of his other arm.

"Hey, you guys! What are you doing?" Stumpy muttered, beginning to get frightened.

We dragged him over to the wall of lockers and Goose lifted the latch and threw a locker door open. We shoved Stumpy inside and slammed the door shut. Then, we slid a pencil through the lock so he couldn't jimmy it open from the inside. Stumpy was trapped.

"Well, Steve, let's go home," said Goose.

"Okay, Goose, let's go," I called out, making sure I said it loud enough for Stumpy to hear.

"Hey, you guys, don't leave me in here. Lemme out!" He sounded really scared. We could hear him squirming inside the locker, but it was no use. He was trapped.

We both pretended to leave the Student Union, but really stood by the doorway watching and laughing. We could hear Stumpy struggling against the locker, wiggling around.

Then we let him out. And Goose and I laughed and told him how much fun it was and that we were just kidding around and we slapped him on the back and then we all sat down to finish the card game.

That was the first of many lock-ups. Each time we left him in there a little longer. Or banged on the sides of the locker a little louder. Or poked stuff in those ventilation holes at the bottom of the locker. Or pushed in the sides of the adjoining lockers to squish him.

Stumpy never struggled. He never fought back. He never returned our insults. And when we let him out, he'd just said, "Okay, you guys. Okay, you guys. Things are cool."

things were not cool

Then came the day in March when Goose and I were really bored. We knew that just locking Stumpy in the locker wouldn't be enough fun. So that day, after we stuck him in the locker, we blew pencil shavings in the top ventilation holes and then poured water down into the locker.

"How's the weather in there, Stumpy?" Goose called.

I stood there laughing so hard my gut hurt.

"Okay, you guys. Okay, you guys," a muffled voice said. "Lemme out."

Finally, right before class, we let him out and whacked him on the back and laughed.

"Just kidding around there, Stumpy," said Goose, gathering up his books. He headed toward the door and I turned to get my books. And that's when I happened to glance at Stumpy's face.

His eyes were bloodshot. As hard as he was trying to hide it, I could tell that not all the wetness on his face had come from the water we'd poured down the back of the locker. And for some reason that day, he didn't look away. He just stood there. And, in that moment, I looked into his eyes.

In that brief instant, in those sad eyes, I saw the real Stumpy. It was as if I could peer down inside him and know what he was feeling. And I heard the cry of his heart: *Care about me. Tell me I matter. I just wish somebody would tell me I matter.*

Then he turned away, shaking. He drew one arm across his face to dry his eyes, grabbed his books, and looked back at me laughing a wild desperate laugh. "Okay, you guys," he said. "Things are cool."

But I knew things were not cool. Not inside Stumpy.

I spent less and less time in the Student Union after that day. Occasionally, I'd walk by the door and see Goose in there slapping Stumpy on the back, laughing. And sometimes Stumpy would see me standing in the doorway, watching. And then he would look away from me, and when I couldn't see his face, he would laugh. But even from across the room I knew it wasn't real laughter.

I never apologized to Stumpy. I never asked for his forgiveness. The memory of that day in the Student Union still haunts me. I can still see his pleading eyes and hear him hiding behind that lonely laughter.

And I can still hear him say, "Okay, you guys. Okay, you guys. Things are cool." But beneath it all I know he was begging me to stop. To listen. To care. To see past the grungy clothes and the acne and the greasy hair. To be the one person who would call him Mark instead of Stumpy.

what's the point?
have you met him?

Since then I've met lots of "Stumpys," each with a different name and a different face. But if you look close enough, their eyes are the same. They feel alone and afraid and they're willing to do anything to hear someone say, "You matter to me. I care about you." They reach out again and again for the hand that slaps them, because without that hand they'd have nothing at all.

Maybe you've met someone like Stumpy. Maybe you know someone like Stumpy. I'll bet—if you're honest with yourself—you'd have to admit there have been times in your life when you've known exactly how he felt.

I wish I could whisper a message back through the years. I wish I could tell him, "I'm sorry, Mark. You *do* matter. You don't deserve this. I care. But more importantly, so does God. He wants to be your friend. He wants to take away the pain, the loneliness and the fear. He loves you, Mark, and you don't have to be alone any more."

"Lord, you know the hopes of the helpless. Surely you will listen to their cries and comfort them. You will bring justice to the orphans and the oppressed, so people can no longer terrify them" *(Psalm 10:17, 18).*

Before you can begin smelling like God, you gotta meet him. And the amazing truth is: God is already waiting to meet you.

More than anything else, God is love. He cares about everyone. Stumpy. Your friends. Me. And you. No matter what you look like, how you dress, or how you act, God cares about you. He cares about your choices and dreams and feelings and heartaches. Everything you do matters to him. And God wants to have a relationship with you.

The world looks at how you dress, what you do, and what you own: *Stuff* + *status* = *success!* But God looks at who you are underneath, in your heart. And he sees all the hopes, struggles, questions, mistakes, hurts and doubts. And he loves you anyway. With a love that will never fail or fade or falter or slip away or grow cold.

You are precious to God.

> *"Give all your worries and cares to God, for he cares about what happens to you" (1 Peter 5:7).*

God doesn't look at the outward appearance—the color of your skin, the new prom dress, the makeup, the muscles, the body piercings, the hairstyle—he looks at what no one else sees . . . the heart.

Some of the Stumpys of this world give up on life. They stop trusting people. They insulate themselves against love and wander through life all alone. Some take their own lives. They figure, "No one will miss me when I'm gone, so why go on living?" They overdose on drugs or slit their wrists. Some fight back. You hear about them on the news. They're the ones who bring guns to school and lash out at the world.

But all the while, God is reaching out for them. For us. For you. So that they can come to know him. So that you can come to know him. And trust in him. And spread the fragrance of his love into the world.

what God was willing to pay

I remember seeing this TV commercial for silver dollars. Some company was selling silver dollars for $39.95 plus $5.95 for shipping and handling. These weren't old or rare coins. Just normal silver dollars. That's $45.90 for a silver dollar worth . . . one dollar. People were paying $45.90 to have $1 shipped to their homes.

I have to admit, at first I thought anyone who would buy a $1 coin for $45.90 was a complete idiot. But then I figured that maybe those coins were worth more to them than to the rest of us.

And I realized that day that *the true worth of an object is not determined by how much someone says it's worth, but by how much someone will actually pay to get it.* By themselves, those coins weren't worth very much, but since people were willing to spend nearly $50 for them, the coins were more valuable than they first appeared.

If that's true, how much are you worth to God?

What was God willing to pay . . . for you?

To God, you are worth more than life itself. You are worth the blood of Jesus Christ. You are worth dying for. Jesus died because he loved you so much he couldn't stand the thought of spending eternity without you: *"For God so loved the world that he gave his only Son, so that everyone who believes in him will not perish but have eternal life" (John 3:16).*

God's love is not based on your inherent worth. You haven't earned his love or deserved it in any way. His love is *unmerited* love. And your worth doesn't come from what you've done or what you look like or what you wear. It's not based on your appearance or performance, where you live or what kind of car you drive. Your worth comes from how much God was willing to pay to restore your severed relationship with him.

maximum love

On May 14, 1999—the week before the release of George Lucas's film *Episode I: The Phantom Menace*—USA TODAY ran a story on the Star Wars movies. In the interview, George Lucas explained that his movies are "a way of saying that it's something to think about and it's something to ask questions about the great mysteries: 'Why are we here?' 'Is there anybody or anything out there that has a relationship to us?' 'Where do we go when we die?' These are good things to ponder."

If you've asked those questions, if you've ever felt alone or wondered if there is anyone out there who cares, the answer is "YES!" No matter who you are. No matter what you've done. God cares about you. He accepts you "as is" and he loves you.

God demonstrated his love for you by sending Jesus. *"Now, no one is likely to die for a good person, though someone might be willing to die for a person who is especially good. But God showed his great love for us by sending Christ to die for us while we were still sinners" (Romans 5:7, 8).*

See? Someone actually gave his life because he loved you so much.

"God loves you dearly, and he has called you to be his very own people" (Romans 1:7).

There is nothing you can do to make God love you more, and nothing you can do to make him love you less. His love is already maxed out. *"The LORD is kind and merciful, slow to get angry, full of unfailing love" (Psalm 145:8).*

Most of the time we try to feel good about ourselves by comparing ourselves to other people: "At least I'm not as fat as she is," "Yeah, he's got game, but I could take him if we played one on one," "I wish I was as tall/ short/fast/strong/cute/sexy/pretty/popular/tough . . . as she/he is."

That's why, when you get a test back, the first thing you do is turn to someone else and ask, "What did you get?" You want to see how you measure up. It's all part of the comparison game.

But God dances with the outcast. Jesus hung out with the Stumpys of his day. His closest friends weren't the religious leaders, but a group of unschooled fishermen those leaders made fun of! And one of Jesus' favorite things to do was to go to parties with prostitutes and thieves.

Why? Because he loved them. And he thought they were worth dying for.

God thinks *you* are worth dying for. Not because of great things you've done, but because of his *deep love for you*.

spiritual incense one
you matter to God

There are lots of Stumpys out there. At your school. In your class. In your church. In your mirror. And God wants them all to know how much they matter to him. He wants you to know how much you matter to him. On the outside we all look different, but in the end we are searching for the same thing—a relationship that won't let us down.

If you already know Jesus, would you help me find the Stumpys? Would you help me get them the message that they matter to God? There's no better way to smell like God than that.

And if you've never met God personally, keep reading. It's no mistake you've picked up this book. God has a message he wants to whisper to your heart. Listen carefully. Let him speak to you and call your name.

Let him reach down into your life and unlock the door. And set you free.

"Do not be afraid, for I have ransomed you. I have called you by name; you are mine" (Isaiah 43:1).

meet the God who is out to get you

What's God like anyhow? Does he even exist? How can I know if God is real?

When I was 15 years old, I got caught shoplifting.

The only problem was, I hadn't actually stolen anything.

My mom dropped me off at the mall. "I'll meet you at the grocery store in 15 minutes!" she said. It was right across the parking lot.

"Okay," I said, "See ya."

I walked inside one of the megastores and headed for the electronics department. One of my favorite bands had just released a new project and I was gonna pick up a copy of it. But once I got there, I spent a little too much time browsing.

Finally, I found the CD, took it to that department's checkout counter and handed over my money. The lady gave me a receipt, I stuffed it into my pocket, and headed outside.

falsely accused!

That's when I glanced at my watch and realized I was supposed to have met my mom like 15 minutes ago. *Oh, man! I better hurry!*

I started jogging across the parking lot when I heard a voice: "Hey, you! Stop!"

I didn't even think the person was yelling at me, so I just kept running.

"Hey!" the voice was louder and closer this time. The guy sounded mad. I turned around and saw this bearded guy sprinting after me.

"This is mall security. Stop right there!"

"What's wrong?"

"Did you just leave that store?"

"Yeah. So?" Now my heart was starting to hammer away inside my chest. *What did I do?*

The guy pointed to the bag I was carrying. "What's in there?"

"Just a CD."

"Let's see." He grabbed the plastic bag containing my new CD. And then he got really serious and he said, "So, do you have anything else that you took from our store without paying for it?"

What kind of a trick question is that? If I say "yes," I get in trouble! If I say "no," I get in trouble! Either way I'd be admitting to stealing! Whatever happened to "innocent until proven guilty"?!

"I paid for this!" I blurted. "I didn't do anything wrong!"

The security guard put his hand on my shoulder and said, "We'll see about that. Come with me."

"I'm supposed to be meeting my mom," I said. It was true.

"Yeah right."

What's going on?! This isn't fair!

For a moment I thought about pulling free and making a break for the grocery store to meet my mom. I knew I could outrun this guy. But how would that look? I'd probably just get in worse trouble!

When we got back to the store, one of the checkout ladies at the front pointed at me. "That's him. That's the one I saw leaving with the CD."

"I bought this in the electronics department!" I said.

They didn't believe me until I pulled out the receipt. Finally, I convinced them, met up with my mom, and headed home.

But my view of that store changed. I couldn't shake the feeling that the people there were out to get me. And I didn't want anything to do with people like that.

what is God like?

Some people think of God that way. They don't want anything to do with him because they think he is out to get them. Like some kind of cosmic security guard, patrolling the universe, always on the look-out to catch them doing something wrong or accuse them of breaking the law. No one could love a god like that. You'd keep your distance and just try to stay out of his way.

Other people think God is too nice to ever punish anyone, like a kindly old grandpa who takes you out for ice cream no matter how you act. But with all the evil in the world, that kind of a god would have to be a weakling and a wimp. I could never respect a god like that.

So what is God really like?

Well, the Bible reveals that God is much more loving (and menacing) than you'd ever expect. You can respect him because he punishes evil. And you can love him because he gives without expecting anything in return. He is real. He is powerful. He is on your side.

But he is out to get you.

worshiping the unknown God

Saul grew up believing in God, but when he met Jesus Christ, a radical change took over his life. He went from being the worst sinner ever (1 Timothy 1:15) to being one of the most influential Christians in history. He spent the rest of his life telling people about Jesus and God's plan for their lives. It was such a radical change he even changed his name from "Saul" to "Paul."

One time, when he visited Athens, Greece, he found idols all around the city. That made him pretty upset. So, he started talking with the leading philosophers of his time. Pretty soon, he was invited to address the most elite group of thinkers in all the world—the council of philosophers on Mars Hill.

That day, Paul said: *"Men of Athens, I notice that you are very religious, for as I was walking along I saw your many altars. And one of them had this inscription on it—'To an Unknown God.' You have been worshiping him without knowing who he is, and now I wish to tell you about him . . ." (Acts 17:22, 23).* Take a look at the chart on page 175 to see what Paul said, and what that has to do with us, today.[1]

Notice that in his speech Paul didn't try to prove that God exists. Actually, the Bible never attempts to prove God's existence. It simply assumes that the concept of God will be reasonable to anyone who is seriously seeking truth. Paul points out in Romans 1:20, *"From the time the world was created, people have seen the earth and sky and all that God made. They can clearly see his invisible qualities—his eternal power and divine nature. So they have no excuse whatsoever for not knowing God."* There's enough evidence in the created world to confirm God's existence.

Paul didn't get on their case for their idol worship. He just used it as a springboard to share with them the truth about God's character, and God's desire for a personal relationship. And Paul didn't beat around the bush. He clearly spoke the truth and let his listeners decide what to do with the message. Paul zeroed in on the uniqueness of the Christian message by pointing to the resurrection.

God is bigger than you think

There is only one God. Powerful. In charge of the universe. And caring. He's the God Paul met. He's the God who *"is not far from any one of us" (Acts 17:27).*

God reveals himself to us through the Bible where he is described in three distinct ways: (1) as the Father who makes us and desires to have a relationship with us; (2) as the Spirit who reveals truth to us and gives spiritual life; and (3) as the Son (Jesus) who actually became one of us to open the way to Heaven to all who would believe.

Christians say there are three "Persons" in one God. Not three gods, but one God. Not three parts to God, but each is distinctively the one true God. We can understand it and explain it . . . but not totally comprehend it. Which is kinda cool. If God were too easy to explain and understand, I'd think maybe someone just made him up.

God is eternal (Psalm 41:13), invisible (Colossians 1:15), perfect (Matthew 5:48), present everywhere (Psalm 139:7-12), all-knowing (Psalm 147:5), holy (Leviticus 11:44) and, best of all, God is love (1 John 4:16). But God is so much bigger than even the best explanation and definition. Like an iceberg, we glimpse only the tip. And God goes down so much deeper.

"Oh, what a wonderful God we have! How great are his riches and wisdom and knowledge! How impossible it is for us to understand his decisions and his methods! For who can know what the Lord is thinking? Who knows enough to be his counselor?" (Romans 11:33, 34).

Before you can learn how to smell like God, you gotta get to know him. Not just learn more *about* him, but actually meet God and get to know him personally. Like Paul did. The security guard incident showed me what injustice can feel like. But our God is just. Because of that he doesn't wink at sin. And he doesn't accuse falsely. He takes wrongdoing seriously. And because of his tremendous love for us, he decided to suffer sin's consequences himself, in our place. That's what the cross is all about.

Paul's speech in Acts 17 is like God's resumé. It gives us the specifics, but now, to really get to know him, we need to meet him on a personal level. Through Jesus: *"And this is the way to have eternal life—to know you, the only true God, and Jesus Christ, the one you sent to earth" (John 17:3).*

spiritual incense two
God is holy and perfect

God is almighty, all-knowing, fair, and full of love. He wants to have a relationship with you. He's out to get you—not to catch you doing something wrong—but to meet you and make you part of his family.

There's a problem, though. Something has gotten between you and God. Let's take a look at what it is and what God wants to do about it.

bad news on backbone rock

So what if I sometimes do stuff that's wrong? I'm a pretty good person. Besides, I'm better than most people. Why can't God just accept me the way I am?

I didn't actually hear the thud.

All I heard were the shouts of fellow rock climbers. I could see a crowd gathering at the base of a nearby cliff. Wondering if someone was making a difficult move as he scaled up Backbone Rock, I walked over to investigate.

"What happened, Aaron?" I called to my partner, one of six of us on a rock climbing training weekend from Doe River Gorge, an outdoor ministry center in eastern Tennessee.

"Someone fell. I saw him drop 80 feet," Aaron replied, pointing across the road. A cluster of people frantically scurried around the base of a nearby climb.

Backbone Rock is a popular site in western Virginia for both rock climbing and rappelling—lowering yourself down a cliff by having your rope pass through a friction-creating device known as a descender. I remembered seeing, earlier that afternoon, a group of college students rappelling Australian-style. They were running off the cliff and then safely slowing their descent before touching the ground. This procedure isn't dangerous when performed properly, but they were rappelling without a belayer, a person to secure the rope in case of an emergency. Apparently, one of them had lost control and had fallen the entire distance to the rocky ground at the base of the cliff.

"i'm okay! leave me alone!"

A few years earlier I'd been trained as a "First Responder" to perform first aid in emergency situations. I decided to head over and see if I could help. Cautiously, I approached the scene of the accident wondering what gruesome sight awaited me at the base of the cliff.

By the time I arrived, a search and rescue team that had been practicing nearby had already responded. They surrounded the injured man and offered their help.

The leader of the rescue team was leaning over the fallen climber. "What's your name, sir?"

"Matt. And I don't need your help. I'm okay."

"You just fell nearly 80 feet. You're hurt. We can help you, Matt."

"Look, I know I've got a broken leg, but that's all. Leave me alone."

It was quite obvious that Matt's right leg was broken. It was bent awkwardly off to the side, not at the knee, but in the middle of his thigh.

"But you could have internal injuries," one of the rescuers replied, fumbling with a first-aid kit the size of a large suitcase. "Wait, Matt! Don't turn your head! Your neck could be broken!"

"But I need to spit," he replied. To the shock of the rescue crew, Matt twisted his head and heaved a mouthful of blood and spit into the dirt.

In addition to the broken leg, he also had a severe head injury. Dark blood oozed from a gaping wound on his scalp. After a fall like that, he almost certainly had internal injuries and probably a broken neck or back. Any movement at all could leave him dead or paralyzed for life. Very few people even survive falls that severe.

The disagreements between the rescuers and Matt escalated. Matt wanted to spit, they wanted him to lay still. Matt wanted to be left alone, they wanted to treat his injuries. Finally, Matt started cussing and swearing at the members of the rescue team. The frustrated leader of the team lost his patience and called off the rest of the squad. "If he refuses treatment, we can't help him. It's the law."

a second chance

Matt lay alone and insisted on rolling himself over. Two members of my climbing party, Ryan Vernon, a Wilderness First Responder, and Karen Maughon, an emergency room nurse, leaned over the man.

"Sir, let us help you. We don't want you to die today," Ryan spoke, trying to calm Matt down.

"I'm not gonna die."

"Please, Matt," Karen implored.

Finally, he allowed us to at least offer the minimal assistance that we could.

In the next few minutes, Karen supported Matt's leg and took his vital signs. Ryan held a bandage to his head to stop the bleeding and to immobilize his neck. I handed them equipment from Ryan's first-aid hip pack.

And all the while that Matt lay there in pain, he tried to convince us he was fine. We realized by then that he had alcohol on his breath. Between being half-dead and half-drunk he wasn't thinking clearly. He insisted on rolling back and forth. Each time he moved, Ryan and I cringed. We both knew that with any movement he could die in our arms. Karen tried to gently speak to Matt of God's love. He said oh yeah he believed in God in one breath and then cursed him with the next. He made it pretty clear to us that he didn't believe in Jesus the same way we did.

Matt cussed and swore and complained. "I only have a broken leg and a bump on my head. I don't have any internal injuries!"

How could anyone be so blind to his own internal condition?

Even when the ambulance arrived and the paramedics loaded him onto a backboard and carried him toward the waiting vehicle, I heard

Matt loudly demanding that he was okay. The last I saw of him, he was arguing with the medical crew, cursing the help they gave.

Later we found out that Matt had actually broken both legs. He was treated for his injuries and, miraculously, was released from the hospital after only a few days.

God had given him a second chance, not only at this life, but at the one to come.

what's the point?

"For all have sinned; all fall short of God's glorious standard" (Romans 3:23).

When I think of how Matt acted, I think of all those who continue to reject God, even when he offers them chance after chance. The heart that refuses to acknowledge its condition before God responds the same way Matt did:

"I'm not hurt! I'm okay the way I am."

"I don't need your help, God. Leave me alone! I know what's best."

"There's nothing wrong with me. It feels all right when I act this way, so it won't hurt me."

All the while eternal death lies only a heartbeat away. And sin is causing injuries that only the grace of God can heal. Matt almost stepped off that cliff and plummeted into unchangeable eternity. But God gave him another shot at life.

Even though God loves us, we've each done things that separate us from experiencing true intimacy with him. We've disobeyed God. The Bible calls it sin. And no matter how hard we try, we can't clean up our lives enough to earn, flatter, or bribe our way into Heaven. It takes a change of heart to make us right before God. And even that's a gift from him.

Most people tumble through this life continually raging against God. They lay helpless, like Matt, cursing and spitting and fighting off every offer of mercy. Before the Holy Spirit enters our hearts, we're all God's enemies, hostile and demanding to be left alone by God. But he comes to our side and we hear these words: *"I am the resurrection and the life. Those who believe in me, even though they die like everyone else, will live again. They are given eternal life for believing in me and will never perish[2] . . . God did not send his Son into the world to condemn it, but to save it. There is no judgment awaiting those who trust him. But those who do not trust him have already been judged for not believing in the only Son of God[3] . . . All who believe in God's Son have eternal life. Those who don't obey the Son will never experience eternal life, but the wrath of God remains upon them."[4]*

big sins and little sins

Sin stinks to God.

Plain and simple. Since God's fragrance is pure and holy, nothing sinful can be in his presence. Each of us sins and our personal sin separates us from experiencing true intimacy with God. And it's not just the big things like murder or rape that stink to God. All those little things we do that we don't tell anyone about, reek as well:

- *Spreading a few words of juicy gossip*
- *Cussing under your breath when things don't go your way*
- *Harboring a grudge against someone at school*
- *Copying a couple of answers for your homework*
- *Checking out those porno websites you heard about*
- *Taking that second, lingering look as she walks away*
- *Telling a few "white lies" to protect your reputation*
- *Complaining to your friends about your parents*
- *Telling yourself it's okay to feel jealous "just this once"*
- *Desiring someone else's looks, brains, or athletic ability*

"You spread out our sins before you—our secret sins—and you see them all" (Psalm 90:8).

We think they're little things. But to God, *all* sin is repulsive. And none of us can measure up to God's perfect standard of holiness. Even our best efforts at pleasing God aren't good enough: *"We are all infected and impure with sin. When we proudly display our righteous deeds, we find they are but filthy rags. Like autumn leaves, we wither and fall. And our sins, like the wind, sweep us away" (Isaiah 64:6).*

Our sins sweep us away. Away from God and into heartache and sadness and loneliness and frustration. And into death. *"For the wages of sin is death, but the free gift of God is eternal life through Christ Jesus our Lord" (Romans 6:23).*

Sinning isn't just what evil people do. It's what all people do when we act, think or speak in ways that don't honor God.

You see, the Ten Commandments weren't given so that we could somehow keep them and earn our way into Heaven. They were given to reveal the depth of our sin. *"For no one can ever be made right in God's sight by doing what his law commands. For the more we know God's law, the clearer it becomes that we aren't obeying it" (Romans 3:20).*

you shouldn't say *shouldn't*?!

When I was working as a wilderness guide, I had an evaluation with my supervisor, Karen. During the evaluation, I mentioned several things I should have done differently on the last course.

But Karen just shook her head, "You shouldn't say shouldn't," she said.

"I shouldn't say shouldn't?"

"That's right."

"But what if I do something wrong?"

"There are no such things as mistakes, only lessons," she said.

On the surface, Karen's philosophy sure sounded nice: *There are no mistakes, only lessons. Humans never do anything wrong. We just go through life facing choices and learning from the consequences of our actions. Therefore, we don't need to feel guilty about anything. Or apologize. Or ask for forgiveness. We're not morally responsible for anything we do. We don't answer to anyone. So just do your best. Live and learn and enjoy the process!*

Sounds good, huh?

But think about it. If Karen were right, then Nazi concentration camps were only "a lesson," rapists wouldn't be doing anything wrong, and torturing children and having sex with your parents would be totally acceptable.

Disgusting, huh? It's ridiculous to even think that way. So why did Karen, and why do so many other people, think like that?

Because admitting that you've actually done something wrong requires you to ask for forgiveness. That means truly humbling yourself. And most people would rather make excuses than be that honest. So we say: "I'm only human!" "It's not that big of a deal!" "I'm better than most people!"

Instead of saying: "You're right, God, I sinned. Please forgive me."

getting rid of guilt

In our imperfect world people deal with guilt in different ways. Some people try to ignore it, but the guilt eats away at their consciences. Some try to run from it, but deep down the guilt always catches up with them. Some try to deny it even exists, but the guilt never quite gets buried deep enough in their hearts. Some try to make up for their wrongs, but the scale never gets balanced out. Some people try to just live with it, and they carry a burden that drains them of joy and offers no escape.

Denying, ignoring, or minimizing your sin won't solve the problem. The guilt doesn't go away. And that burden of regrets is still there.

So how *can* we get rid of all this excess baggage?

God won't let you run or hide or bury or make up for your sin. The punishment has already begun in your heart. Instead, he wants you to be free and he offers to take away the guilt by taking away the sin.

"I confessed all my sins to you and stopped trying to hide them. I said to myself, 'I will confess my rebellion to the LORD.' And you forgave me! All my guilt is gone" (Psalm 32:5).

Turn to God and accept the forgiveness he freely offers. God promises to take your wrongs upon himself, forgive them, and forget them. Forever.

spiritual incense three
sin separates people from God

Part of getting to know God is getting to know yourself and being honest about who you truly are. And how much your life apart from God stinks.

Matt should have died that day. Instead, he was given a second chance. A new life. That's called mercy. And that's the kind of mercy God specializes in.

Have you ever heard God's words and rejected them? Have you denied your sins and demanded to help yourself, to do things your own way? Without God's grace, our situation is hopeless. Just like it was for Matt. But Matt got a replay. That's what grace is all about.

If you've never confessed your sinfulness to God, you can do it right now. If you've never placed your faith in Christ, you can accept his offer of eternal life before you even turn the page.

"If we say we have no sin, we are only fooling ourselves and refusing to accept the truth. But if we confess our sins to him, he is faithful and just to forgive us and to cleanse us from every wrong" (1 John 1:8, 9).

It's not too late. Listen to God's call. Accept his offer. Trust in his love. Don't step off the cliff of this life into uncertainty—fall instead into God's waiting and forgiving arms.

i own the future!

Why did Jesus have to come to earth, anyway? Why did he have to die? And what difference does his life way back then make to my life today?

When I was 16 years old, I passed the test—on my second try.

The lady behind the desk handed me a small plastic card with my name and address, my pimple-faced picture, and the tiny words "Wisconsin State Driver's License." I held that little card up to the light and thought, *This is my passport to freedom. This is my ticket to adventure. I own the future!*

"no problem, dad!"

That night I strolled into the living room and asked, "Dad, can I borrow the car?"

For two weeks he couldn't say "no" fast enough.

Finally, a month later, on November 16, he sighed, "Where do you want to go?"

"Whitewater," I said. It was a town about 45 minutes away—I figured I'd start small and work my way up. Whitewater had the closest college that offered open gym late at night. And since I was addicted to basketball, I wanted to check it out.

"Let me talk to your mother."

They met in the living room. Finally, I was called in. My dad cleared his throat. "Son, your mother and I have been talking . . . we think it's time you had a little more responsibility—"

By now he'd pulled out the car keys. I was drooling. He was swinging them slowly back and forth through the air . . . it was hypnotizing . . .

You are getting very responsible . . .

Yes, master . . .

"—I'll let you borrow the car under two conditions. First, you must be back by midnight. And, second, out in the country there's a stop sign in the middle of nowhere, it just sort of pops up at you . . . drive carefully and don't miss that sign."

"Yes, master . . . I mean . . . of course, no problem, Dad! Gimme a break! I'm 16 years old! Look, I've got my license right here!" I whipped out my crisp, brand-new driver's license. Then I snatched those keys from his fingers, held them up to the light and said, "My passport to freedom! My ticket to adventure! I own the future!"

I hopped into the car. Now, when you first learn to drive, they teach you to have two hands on the wheel positioned at 9:00 and 3:00 as if the steering wheel were a clock. Then you have to check your seatbelt, side-view mirror, speedometer, rearview mirror . . .

Seatbelt, side-view, speedometer, rearview . . .

Seatbelt, side-view, speedometer, rearview . . .

. . . all the while maneuvering through traffic and not taking your eyes off the road. Well, about two weeks after you get your license you start driving with your left arm hanging out the window, one finger on the steering wheel, and the only things you pay much attention to are your date and the volume on the stereo.

I was at that stage the night I drove to Whitewater.

All I could think of was playing hoops. I wasn't really too focused on my driving skills.

Sure, I came to the stop sign—no problem. I stopped. I looked left, looked right, looked left again. No cars. No problem. What was my dad worried about anyway? I continued to the gym.

For two hours I played three-on-three and shot free throws. Finally, at 11:10 P.M. I left the gym with plenty of time to make it home by midnight. Or so I thought.

Now I should tell you, it wasn't my fault. It really wasn't. While I'd been in the gym, fog had settled in the valley between Whitewater and that stop sign. I had the stereo turned up, arm hanging out the window, one finger on the steering wheel, when I heard this loud grinding noise. I thought it was the bass part in the song I was listening to. I'm like, "Cool!" I turned up the radio. A few seconds later, I heard it again. "All right! This song is awesome!" I cranked the radio even louder.

Only when I saw the stop sign whip past the car did I realize that the grinding sound was made by driving over those grooves in the pavement that are there to warn you that a stop sign is coming.

Uh, oh.

a long ride home

I slammed on the brakes and screeched to a stop in the middle of the intersection.

I looked left, looked right, looked left again. No cars.

Whew.

Oh well, I'll stop twice at the next one!

And then, as I pulled back onto the road, I looked up into the rearview mirror. One pair of headlights was visible, even through the fog. It was the only headlights I'd seen all night. *Huh, wouldn't it be funny if that was a cop car?*

Siren. Lights. Siren. Lights. Siren. Lights.

It was a cop car and it wasn't funny.

The police officer pulled me over and walked up to my window, "Can I see your license son?"

I gulped, glanced at my watch and pulled out the plastic card.

As he looked at my license I could almost hear him thinking, *This feels pretty new, boy!* Finally he asked, "Did you see that stop sign back there?"

"Um . . . that one right there?"

"Yes."

"Um . . . do you mean just a few minutes ago or a few hours ago coming from the other direction? Because I know I saw it then . . ."

"Just a few—Look. I'm gonna have to give you a ticket."

He took my new driver's license back to his patrol car and wrote out my ticket. It seemed like it took him about fourteen hours to write down my name. Time was ticking away . . . my life was ticking away.

Finally, he returned and handed me the ticket. It was for about six zillion dollars more than I had on hand.

All the way home I drove with my hands at 9:00 and 3:00 checking my seatbelt, side-view, speedometer, rearview . . . I stopped about 15 times at every stop sign on the way, just to be sure.

As I drove up the driveway, it was 1:15 A.M. I knew my dad was gonna kill me. But when I saw that there were no lights on in the house, my confidence returned.

He must have gone to bed! Yessssss! He'll never find out . . . I own the future!

Quietly, I opened the door and began tiptoeing through the kitchen. Just one more room and I'd be in my bedroom, home-free.

Suddenly, a voice cut through the night, "Steven James!"

"Ahh!" I jumped into the air higher than I had all night playing hoops.

"Dad! What are you doing sitting in the dining room . . . in the dark?"

"I wasn't sleepy. Do you know what time it is?"

"Ah, well, I know it's late," I yawned as convincingly as I could. "Listen, Dad, I better be getting to bed, I have school tomorrow. See you in the morning." I started toward my room.

"It is morning."

"Oh."

"What happened, young man?"

Oh, man. He had me.

the gift

What could I do? He'd caught me and I knew it. Even worse, he knew it. I didn't know what to say. There was no escape. I had to tell him the truth. "Um, Dad, listen. I was driving home and I came to that stop sign and . . ." I paused to see how I was doing. He was staring at me silently through the darkness. I could hear the old grandfather clock ticking rhythmically.

Tick, tock. Tick, tock.

"Okay, Dad, look, I didn't stop in time at the stop sign. I got a ticket." I set the ticket down on the table in front of my dad.

For a long time I stood there in the darkness of our dining room. My dad didn't say a word.

Tick, tock. Tick, tock.

I started thinking, *Maybe he fell asleep and I'm off the hook!*

That's when he spoke. "Steve, I'm disappointed in you. I warned you about that stop sign and you didn't listen." He picked up the ticket and then continued, "Whoa! This ticket is for about six zillion dollars more than you have on hand . . . Listen, tomorrow, I'll pay off this ticket and—"

"Dad, I'll pay you back every penny! Just give me time."

He paused for a minute, "You can start paying me back at the end of the week."

I didn't sleep much that night. It wasn't the fact that I'd broken the law that really bothered me. That I could live with. It was the fact that I'd disappointed my dad. I'd let him down. I'd failed him. He'd given me responsibility, trust, and freedom—and I'd blown it.

The end of that week, and the next, and the next week came. I'd hardly paid off a fraction of the ticket when Christmas arrived.

After church, we opened presents and as I was cleaning up the living room, I found an unopened card under the tree. It was addressed to me.

Cool, maybe it'll be some money so I can pay back my dad!

I opened up the card and read the inside. It was nothing fancy, just four handwritten words, "Merry Christmas, Love Dad." But what caught my attention was the small slip of paper folded up inside the card. It was my ticket. And written with red magic marker across the top were three words: "PAID IN FULL."

As I sat there amidst the piles of paper and boxes, my thoughts returned to the first Christmas and God's gift to us all took on new meaning to me.

You see, my father had paid off the debt that I owed because of what I'd done wrong when I broke the law. It was a debt so big, I couldn't pay it. So he paid it in full, and forgave me just like our Heavenly Father did so many years ago on that first Christmas. God sent his Son to live in our place and to eventually die in our place to pay off our debt of sin. And you know what? Faith in him is the only passport to freedom, the true ticket to adventure—the one chance to finally and completely own the future.

what's the point?

"But when the right time came, God sent his Son, born of a woman, subject to the law. God sent him to buy freedom for us who were slaves to the law, so that he could adopt us as his very own children" (Galatians 4:4, 5).

When Jesus was born, he became fully human while remaining fully God. *How* he did this is a mystery to us, but *why* he did it is crystal clear. We needed a Savior who could suffer in our place, and pay off our collective debt of sin to God. Only a God-Man could do that.

He was human so he could know our hurts and our pains, our fears and our struggles. He knew what it is like to be cold and tired and alone and afraid. And he was God so he could do something about it. Jesus kept the law in our place. And Jesus allowed himself to be filled with all the hurt in the world—that's what it meant to suffer the penalty of the law.

And then he died. He died because we die and in order to help us he had to be just like us in everything, even death.

But because he was perfect and he was God, death had no claim on him. He came back to life again. And that changed everything. He made our past gone forever. He made our future full of hope. And he made today—this very minute—a special gift. He fills the present with chances to show him how much we love him.

paid in full

The debt we owe God because of what we've done wrong is too big to pay off on our own. That's why Jesus had to come. And when Jesus died on the cross he called out, "It is finished!"—the same words that appeared in those days on bills that had been paid. Everyone who heard what Jesus said must have thought, *He's yelling, "Paid in full!" What's that mean? What debt is he talking about?*

Our debt. Our sin-debt.

Why did Jesus have to die? One Bible verse sums it all up:

"He was handed over to die because of our sins, and he was raised from the dead to make us right with God" (Romans 4:25).

Jesus lived a perfect life in your place, he suffered and died in your place, and he came back from the dead to guarantee that all of God's promises have come true. So that you can receive the gift of eternal life.

what makes heaven a gift?

If someone gives you a $50 check for a birthday present, did you earn it? No. But if your boss hands you a $50 paycheck, did you earn that? Yes. One is a gift, one is payment. One is earned, one is not. One is by grace, the other is by works.

Paul says if we were saved by works—even just a little bit—then we would be earning Heaven and we wouldn't be saved by God's kindness: *"And if they are saved by God's kindness, then it is not by their good works. For in that case, God's wonderful kindness would not be what it really is—free and undeserved" (Romans 11:6).*

It's totally a God thing.

When it comes to Heaven, God picks up the bill. All of it. It's not like he pays for the meal and we cover the tip. It's a gift, free and clear and all the way. God says, "Heaven is on me."

That's what grace is all about.

spiritual incense four
Jesus paid the debt of your sins and rose from the dead to offer you new life

God's grace has no fine print, no hidden costs, no strings attached. It's free and it's ours. And it lasts forever. Guaranteed. We have nothing to offer him in return except an attitude of gratitude and a life of service—learning to smell like him.

"He has removed our rebellious acts as far away from us as the east is from the west. The LORD is like a father to his children, tender and compassionate to those who fear him" (Psalm 103:12, 13).

One passport to freedom. One ticket to adventure. So that you, and I could truly and completely own the future.

after the shots rang out

I've done some bad stuff I've never told anyone about. Can God for-give even those things?

When I first met my friend Crystal Sturgill, she was 19 years old. She'd just started serving her first year of three consecutive life sentences without parole, plus 25 years. She is a convicted mass murderer. Here is her story:

"Joe and Jason had the guns. They all got out of the car and they were stand-ing between the van and the car. And I started crying and slapping Dean's leg, 'Get me outta here.' And he told me, 'They won't do anything.'

Joe came over to us and said, 'They've seen us and they'll call the police. They've all gotta die.'

It wasn't reality anymore."

Crystal paused and looked across the table. Just to her right was a steel-reinforced window. Outside, the prison yard was surrounded by two 12-foot fences laced with cruel-looking curls of barbed wire. She wanted to continue, but the tears welling in her eyes told me how dif-ficult it was for her to relive the memories.

Crystal was soft-spoken and eloquent, hesitant to smile, but genu-ine, kind and trusting. She hadn't moved from her chair since she started telling me her story two hours ago.

"I saw Jason shoot Vidar in the head. Immediately, the man dropped. Mrs. Lillelid was the next to be shot. . . . Then there were a bunch of shots.

Dean pulled my head down. I didn't see anything else. It seemed like they went on forever. Finally, they stopped. I was screaming and crying.

Joe was yelling, 'I can't believe you just did that!'

Everyone was screaming."

"those people die for me every day"

On April 6, 1997, Crystal (18 at the time) and her five friends: Edward Dean Mullins (19), Natasha Cornett (18), Joe Risner (20), Jason Blake Bryant (14), and Karen Howell (17) left their rural Kentucky homes for New Orleans. They thought they'd be back.

They'd already had a wild weekend—drinking, drugs, even self-mutilation. After vandalizing a hotel on Saturday, they got scared of being arrested and decided to head for the state line. One thing led to another, and soon they'd stolen some guns and ammunition.

Things were spinning out of control.

When Joe's car began overheating, they pulled into a rest stop near Baileyton, Tennessee. While they were stretching their legs, Vidar Lillelid, carrying his two-year-old son, Peter, approached the cluster of teens who were dressed in chains, black clothes and black lipstick. Vidar and his family were devout Jehovah's Witnesses. They asked the group if they believed in God.

A few minutes later, his wife Delfina and their six-year-old daughter, Tabitha, joined them. Dean and Crystal didn't want to hear any talk about God, so they went back to wait in Joe's car. But then their friends climbed into the van with the Lillelids and started driving. Dean and Crystal followed in the car.

Kidnapping the family at gunpoint, they drove a few miles away to a deserted dirt road. Then, everyone filed out of the van and stood between the van and the car. Moments later, the family lay in the mud in a pool of blood.

Vidar had been shot six times, Delfina eight times. They died holding their critically-wounded children. Tabitha died the next day; she'd been shot in the head. Peter, who had been shot through the eye, survived.

"We got all our stuff from our bags, then we all got into the van and drove as fast as we could. I heard a thump followed by a cracking sound. Only later did I learn that we had run over their bodies."

At the trial, Natasha, Karen and Joe all testified that Jason was the sole shooter. Jason claimed it was Dean and Joe. All six pleaded guilty. They were all involved.

Crystal remarked, "I couldn't believe it. Those people die for me every day."

"we were the freaks"

The media portrayed them as the "vampire cult," and the "occult teen killers." Pictures of their body piercings and gothic clothes flooded newspapers across the country, and even the world. Bizarre stories of satanic blood-letting rituals sent ripples of horror through Tennessee.

Crystal maintains that they didn't drink blood or worship Satan. But, she says, "We dressed in black so we'd stand out. And we did self-mutilation. We were the freaks, the outcasts. We were interested in books on witches and spells. We were trying to find answers."

Crystal admits that after a while, she and her friends wanted to be the outcasts, but not at first. At first all they wanted was for people to care about them and accept them even though they were different.

"i felt different right away"

Two days after the murders, they were arrested in Arizona and flown back to Tennessee to face 29 criminal charges, including three counts of first-degree murder.

"We got to the jail and there was a mob scene. There were TV cameras and bright lights that hurt my eyes. Someone pushed me and called me Charles Manson's daughter."

She felt completely alone awaiting trial. Even though she'd gone to church, sung in the choir, and even attended youth group, none of it had impacted her deep inside. Crystal had no hope for the future, nowhere to turn. And then she started to open her mail. "All I got was hate mail. My lawyers have boxes of letters. Everyone wrote that they hoped I fried and they wrote, 'the wages of sin is death.' But they left out the last half of the verse, that 'the free gift of God is eternal life through Christ Jesus our Lord.'"[5]

Finally she got a letter from Jack Bruce, a pastor in nearby Elizabethton, Tennessee.

> *Crystal,*
> *I realize that you may feel as if everyone is against you. I want you to know that it is not true. From my study of the Bible, I can assure you that nothing you have ever done, thought or said is so bad that it will keep God from extending to you His forgiveness. No one has strayed too far to be forgiven. He is very willing to welcome you back to Him. I would love to tell you about it.*
> *In Christ's love,*
> *Jack Bruce, Minister*

Those caring words touched Crystal. A couple weeks later she wrote him back and invited him to meet with her. In jail, Pastor Bruce led her to a personal relationship with Jesus Christ. Crystal still remembers the immediate change in her life. "He came in and we talked for a couple of hours. We prayed together. I felt different right away. And over the next few days I read the Bible continuously."

Even now when she talks about the murders, her eyes fill with tears. Crystal wishes there was some way she could have stopped the shootings. She prays regularly for Peter, the little boy who survived.

"My biggest regret is that I didn't come to know Christ sooner. If I had had this personal relationship with him maybe I could have touched my friends and stopped this. That day, I could have talked to them (the Lillelids) about Jesus," she says.

"don't think God won't love you"

Crystal wants teens to know that those in prison and those outside its walls aren't that much different—we're all sinners in need of God's grace. "Don't think God won't love you if you've done something," she says. "He loves us with our faults. He knows that we can't be perfect and he'll blot out all our transgressions. . . . God doesn't love me any less than he loves you and he doesn't love the preacher any more than he loves me."

She also wants Christian teens to share God's love, especially with the unlovable. "Don't judge people. . . . Don't judge those who are different from you, reach out to them with God's love. We were the freaks, look past that to the soul that would fight in Jesus' army."

When she and her friends pleaded guilty, the death sentence was waived in lieu of three consecutive life sentences without the possibility of parole. Her case is under appeal, and Crystal hopes that one day she will be released from prison. "I think that God has more for me than this, but if not I pray that I'll serve him wherever I'm at. If I touch just one person in this place, then I've done a miracle."

Crystal now faces the future with hope. God has turned her life completely around. Even though she is imprisoned, her soul has been set free.

If you don't have that kind of freedom, if your soul is alone or afraid or filled with regrets and pain, you can find forgiveness for the past and hope for the future by simply trusting in Christ for your salvation.

Just like Crystal did that day, two months after the shots rang out.

what's the point?

"'Come now, let us argue this out,' says the LORD. 'No matter how deep the stain of your sins, I can remove it. I can make you as clean as freshly fallen snow. Even if you are stained as red as crimson, I can make you as white as wool'" (Isaiah 1:18).

There's only one solution to our sin problem—the sin needs to be removed. It's like a stain on your soul that needs to be cleaned off before you can be in the presence of God. What is the ultimate stain-remover? What's the only solution available?

The blood of Jesus.

"But if we are living in the light of God's presence, just as Christ is, then we have fellowship with each other, and the blood of Jesus, his Son, cleanses us from every sin" (1 John 1:7).

God doesn't want to hurt your pride—he wants to kill it! You shouldn't be embarrassed by your sins, you should be horrified. If you're only sorry for doing something wrong because you got caught, your heart hasn't changed. Embarrassment means there is still some pride in you that won't allow you to go all the way and hate your sin.

When you honestly admit your guilt, you're finally free to move on to true forgiveness.

life's most important ingredient

It's been said that humans can live for a month without food, a week without water, five minutes without air—but not for one second without hope. That's why Jesus came—to fill us with hope. To give us something significant to live for and look forward to. Guilt suffocates hope. But he takes away our guilt so he can fill us with hope. Jesus provides the only solution available for our sin problem.

If you look up the word "hope" in a dictionary, you'll see it means "expectation," not "wish." If you hope for something you expect it to happen. You don't just wish that it might. Hope is always linked to trust, faith and expectation:

- Christians don't hope Jesus was raised from the dead, they have hope *because* he was raised.
- We don't hope Jesus will return to take us to Heaven, we have hope *because* he will return.
- We don't hope God will forgive our sins, we have hope *because* he has already forgiven them.
- We don't hope we'll make it into Heaven, we have hope *because*, through faith in Christ, we are *guaranteed* entrance into Heaven.

will God forgive me for this?

The importance of hope became clear to me one night when I met a teenage girl after one of my speaking engagements. I don't know her name, but I'll never forget her face.

She was maybe 16 or 17. Tall, attractive, friendly. She cornered me as I was leaving the comedy club where I'd been performing. "Thanks for talking about forgiveness," she whispered.

"You're welcome," I said. "Any specific reason you mention that?"

Slowly, she pulled her hands out of her jean pockets and held them up. Even in the dim light I could see the thick, blood-stained bandages wrapped around each of her wrists.

"I wonder if God can forgive me for this?" she said, as her eyes filled with tears.

We talked about God's love and forgiveness. I explained that God's love is unfailing, unflinching and everlasting; that his forgiveness is full and free and forever; and that when he forgives, he forgets and doesn't keep a record of wrongs.

"And I will forgive their wickedness and will never again remember their sins" (Jeremiah 31:34).

No matter what bad things you've done, no matter how many times you've done them, God's grace is greater than your sin and his love goes deeper than your failures. He will forgive you and will remember your sins no more.

That's what I told her.

And before she left that night, she told me she'd accepted God's ultimate forgiveness.

spiritual incense five
God offers lasting hope through Jesus Christ, no matter what you've done

Christianity offers a solution to our problems that isn't based on human efforts or achievement, but on God's achievements. The answer to pleasing God lies in a person (Jesus), not a set of rituals or requirements. And hope is available for even the most stranded soul or wounded heart. Christianity answers life's biggest questions:

Guilt: *"What do I do with my guilt for the wrong things I've done?"* God says he will take the guilt upon himself, forgive the wrongs and forget them (Jeremiah 31:34).

Loneliness: *"Where can I turn when I'm lonely?"* God is always nearby when you need him most. He will never abandon you (Hebrews 13:5).

Death: *"What will happen to me when I die?"* God says eternal life awaits all who believe in Jesus as their Savior (John 11:25, 26).

Despair: *"What hope is there when bad things happen?"* God works even bad things out for the ultimate good of his followers (Romans 8:28).

Most philosophies and religions tell people to (1) accept your flaws: "You're only human," (2) deny your flaws: "You're not such a bad person," (3) ignore your flaws: "Just feel good about yourself."

Christianity says, "Admit your flaws and seek forgiveness!"

Christianity isn't a crutch for the weak, it's the answer for the honest. Hope can only come from a renewed heart. From receiving the unearned, undeserved gift of God's love and forgiveness.

We have confidence in God's promises and look forward to seeing them all come true. Crystal does. The girl in the comedy club does. I do.

And you can, too. Through faith.

"May the God of hope fill you with all joy and peace as you trust in him, so that you may overflow with hope by the power of the Holy Spirit" (Romans 15:13, NIV).

trapped 70 feet underground

What does it mean to "turn to God"? Do I have to change my life around before God will accept me? What do I need to do to become acceptable to him?

"Okay, let's get going—it's still a long way out of this cave," I said, scanning the faces of the other cavers. All seven of us were packed like sardines in the tiny three-foot tall cavern. I tipped my mud-encrusted headlamp toward Kilby. "Ladies first."

Julie, Trina, and Kilby wormed their way over the boulder, twisting and stretching their bodies to fit through the tight squeeze called "The Coil."

i can't move!

That's when Walt turned to me, "Hey, can I try going under the boulder?"

To get out of the room, you either had to slide over a boulder lodged in the mouth of the passage, or slither under it through a twisting crack along the floor of the cave.

At least, it looked like you could slither under it. . . . I stared at the passageway, then I looked at Walt's 6'5", 240-pound frame.

"Yeah, why not? Go for it."

Matt and I watched as Walt's torso disappeared beneath the boulder. A minute later he was grunting. "Hey man, I can't move."

"C'mon, you can get it! Try again," said Matt.

After a few more grunts I started getting a little nervous.

"I think I'm stuck, man!" Walt howled, wiggling uselessly against the rock walls of the cave. He was perfectly wedged in the tight passageway.

"What do you mean you're stuck?" Julie called from somewhere beyond, a tremor rising in her voice.

"Stuck! Stuck! I can't move!"

"Just settle down and relax, Walt! Don't get tense—it'll only make it worse. Try exhaling your air and moving forward." I was trying to calm everyone down. But I didn't feel very calm.

Neither did Walt. He was starting to hyperventilate.

"Relax, man! Relax!" I yelled, a little too loudly. "Breathe!"

This was definitely not good. The two boulder tunnels converged into The Coil, which meant that Walt wasn't the only one stuck, Matt and I were sealed in. Walt was blocking the passage. No one could go in or out. And none of the girls had ever been caving before so they wouldn't be able to find their way out to get help. On top of that, we were in a remote, deserted cave in southwestern Wisconsin. Only a handful of people even knew the cave was there. No one would come looking for us.

Finally, Walt calmed down, but he still couldn't move.

All I could do was stare at Walt's big ol' stinky feet blocking my way.

no way out

Time crept by. Seconds. Minutes. Maybe even hours. There was no way of telling.

"Try it again." I was speaking to the soles of Walt's boots. His head was in the next room. "You should be able to wriggle to the left there—I see a gap in the rocks."

"I can't see where you're talking about."

"There you go!" I called as his body inched forward. "You almost got it now!"

Yeah, right.

He was only getting more and more stuck. Walt wasn't going anywhere. None of us were.

At first I'd thought he could make it, now I really didn't know what we were gonna do.

After a while, Walt started shivering. Hypothermia was setting in. The cool, damp rocks were draining his body heat. That was bad news. If we didn't get him out soon, his life could be in danger. Someone needed to do something. Fast.

The girls would have to go for help. Maybe I could call directions to them through the wall of the cave . . .

I heard Kilby talking to Trina, "We're never gonna get back out!"

Suddenly, I had an idea.

"Walt, let me pull you out backwards."

"What?"

"*Back out.* Try to back out, go backwards. If I can pull you back this way, then you can go out the way you came in!"

"That's crazy! If it doesn't work it'll only be harder for me to work my way through!"

It probably took me 15 minutes to convince him it was worth a try. He kept trying to squeeze forward. Finally, he agreed.

Matt and I each grabbed a foot and began to pull. We eased up whenever Walt screamed in pain, then we cranked on his legs again. Pull, grunt, scream, stop. . . . Pull, grunt, scream, stop. . . . We were pulling 240 pounds of jammed Walt uphill.

"He budged! I felt him budge!" Matt called.

Sure enough, a few minutes later Walt was sitting next to us catching his breath and rubbing the bruises on his side.

"We did it man, we're outta here!"

We all eased our way over the boulder, picked our way through the tunnels to the cave entrance, and celebrated with some granola bars and sports drinks.

walking the way of the way

One thing sticks in my mind: If Walt hadn't changed his mind and let that affect his course of action, he'd still be in that cave.

And so would I.

The first step to getting rescued was realizing he couldn't do it on his own. Then he needed to believe the voice of someone he couldn't see and trust in a power other than himself to be set free.

The Bible tells us that because of sin, we're in a hopeless situation, too. We're stuck. We wanna get to Heaven, but trying to get there our way doesn't work. God puts it like this, *"There is a path before each person that seems right, but it ends in death" (Proverbs 14:12)*. It's a dead-end tunnel. The more we push forward doing things our way, the tighter we wedge ourselves in. Sure, the passage looks good at first, but in the end, it's a trap.

The good news is, there is a way out—Jesus. He said it himself, *"I am the way, the truth, and the life. No one can come to the Father except through me" (John 14:6)*.

Not only did Jesus claim there was only one way to Heaven . . . not only did he claim to *know* the way to God . . . he actually claimed to *be* the way! The only way to God. No other religious leader has ever claimed that. They all claim to know a way, if only their followers will follow a certain set of guidelines.

But not Jesus. He said, "You wanna go to Heaven? You wanna meet the Father? Then you gotta come through me." His followers taught the same thing.

After Jesus went back to Heaven, Peter was arrested for healing a man in the name of Jesus. He told the religious leaders, *"There is salvation in no one else! There is no other name in all of heaven for people to call on to save them" (Acts 4:12)*.

In fact, the early followers of Jesus were so convinced that Jesus was the only way to Heaven that they didn't even call themselves Christians. Before believers were called "Christians" they called themselves, "followers of the Way" (Acts 9:1, 2; 22:4; 24:14).

There are loads of religions out there. And some of them are *way* out there. Each has its own "designer-god." And lots of people think that as long as they worship something, it's better than nothing. "Sure, there's a god," they say, "but everyone just worships him differently and calls him by a different name. All roads lead to the same place. All religions lead to Heaven."

Not according to Jesus.

He claimed he was the only way to God and he told the religious leaders, *"Unless you believe that I am who I say I am, you will die in your sins" (John 8:24).*

No one comes to God their own way, you gotta go through Jesus.

a different direction

Repentance is such a key teaching of the Bible that it's important to understand what it is and what it isn't. It's more than just feeling bad about something you did. Or being sorry. Or getting scared of what might happen to you after you get caught. Repentance is even more than admitting you did something wrong.

Repentance means to "change your mind" or "turn around." But it doesn't mean "clean up your life so that God will finally accept you." If it did, we'd all be stuck, doomed to perish in a cave.

Repentance is an admission that you've been going the wrong direction, and that you're willing to change course and let God lead you. We first repent when we trust in Christ, but believers also live a lifestyle of repentance, whenever we find that we're going down the wrong road.

Think of it this way. If you were driving down the highway and you realized you missed your exit, you'd look for a place to pull over and turn around. You'd quickly make a U-turn because, with every passing moment, you're getting farther away from your destination. That's what it's like for us and God. When we repent we make a U-turn to God.

You can't face two directions at once. So turning toward God means turning your back on your old lifestyle. Does that mean you'll never sin again? No, of course not. But you won't be deliberately pursuing sin, constantly justifying sin or fully enjoying sin. Because you've been given a new chance, a new lifestyle and a new direction from God.

did judas repent?

The Bible records the stories of a bunch of people who were sorry for what they did, but didn't actually repent. The most famous is Judas. Before committing suicide, Judas realized that he'd handed an innocent man (Jesus) over to be killed. He was so upset he ran to the priests and admitted his sin. He tried to make it right by giving back the money they'd paid him for his treachery. But when they laughed at him, he went out and killed himself.

Did he feel bad? Yes. Was he sorry? Yes. Did he try to make up for his wrong? Yes. Did it work? No.[6] Because he left God out of the equation. And without God, he was caught in a downward spiral that only led to destruction. With God, he could have been washed clean. Without God he was washed out.

Sure, Judas felt bad about what he'd done. But he wasn't ready to turn to God and ask for forgiveness. And it cost him everything.

Repentance is more than just admitting you've done something wrong. It's the admission that you yourself are all wrong, that your entire life is going in the wrong direction and you're hopeless without God's help.

Repentance only occurs when we reach the place of no excuse and no escape. When we stare at our sinful selves head-on and don't turn away, we're faced with a choice—despair or dependence. Judas chose despair.

Don't make the same mistake he did.

spiritual incense six
repentance means turning to God and letting him change the direction of your life

When we trust in God rather than ourselves, and change our strategy from "getting out my way" to "letting him set me free" he does it all and we can get out alive. But it all starts with admitting that we need his help, then trusting him alone to set us free.

What direction are you heading? What course are you on? Do you ever feel trapped, like there's no way out? Well, in this life, there's only one way out—Jesus. If you haven't found him yet, I hope you do soon.

He's got the greatest celebration of all waiting at the end of the tunnel.

escape from the planet of the living dead

Where will I go when I die? Is there any way I can know for sure I'll go to Heaven?

I never liked my Grandpa.

He sat, alone in the smoke-filled living room, slouched next to his ashtray. The television droned on. The shades were drawn. Only thin slivers of light pierced in from the outside world. And every once in a while, he'd bark out orders or say that the kids oughtta shut up and go somewhere else to play. Not exactly your ideal grandfather.

My parents told us stories about his hunting and fishing days. I saw photos of the deer, the mounted bass on the wall, even the bear rug upstairs, and I wished he'd take me out fishing or teach me to hunt. But he rarely left the couch.

"He doesn't hunt and fish as much any more," my parents said.

Most of his fishing buddies were too old, or too tired, or "weren't around anymore." And Grandpa wasn't interested in making me his new fishing buddy. So my brother, my sister, and I pretty much stayed clear of the living room and explored the rest of the old six-bedroom house.

he found the note

I was a kid back then, so I noticed kid things. I noticed that Grandpa stayed behind when we went to church. He told dirty jokes. And when he said Jesus' name he wasn't praying. I waited for someone to tell him it was wrong, but no one ever did.

Since they didn't, one day I decided I would.

My teacher at the Christian school I attended helped me write the note. At the end of our Easter visit, as everyone else was saying their goodbyes, I slipped the piece of paper under Grandpa's pillow. In that note I wrote that God didn't like it when he said those things, but that God loved him, and so did Jesus and so did I and I wanted him to go to Heaven and so did God—but he needed to love Jesus and believe in him first.

Yeah, maybe I was pretty naïve, but I wasn't sure what else to do. Can you blame me? Deep down, I cared about him.

A few days later Grandma phoned my parents. She said Grandpa had found my note and that she wanted to talk to me. As Mom handed me the phone she mouthed, "What note?"

Excitedly, I took the phone. I expected Grandma to thank me. She told me Grandpa had read the note. But then she said my note had made him worse. "I'll have to start all over trying to get him to go to church. You can put your mother back on now," she finished.

I didn't know anyone had ever tried to get Grandpa to go to church, no one had ever tried when I was around. . . . Why would my note have made him worse? Wouldn't it have helped? I'd thought I was doing the right thing, but now I felt rotten. For a long time I didn't want to chance telling people about Jesus for fear of "making things worse."

the big gulf

We kept visiting them for holidays and stuff. I'd go in, give him this awkward sideways hug, ask him what he was watching and he'd grumble something about the bass fishing show that was on TV and then that was it. We didn't even make eye contact. I never knew what more to say. I wished there were something, anything to talk about. Mostly I drifted into the other room to do my homework.

Even though a big gulf grew between us, I kept praying for him. Because despite everything, I cared about him.

About that time, Grandpa realized he was dying.

Operation after operation made him weaker and weaker. No more smoking now. No more leaving the house. No more walking. Grandma spent all her time taking care of him; shuffling him from the bed to the couch to the bathroom. She read devotions to him now that he didn't complain so much. A local pastor started to visit him.

I don't really know what was going through his head, maybe the Bible stories were making a difference. Maybe we just liked to think that they were. One day Grandma told us that Grandpa believed in Jesus nowadays. "We pray together. He listens to devotions and takes the Lord's Supper," she said.

Months slipped away as Grandpa's world grew smaller and smaller. I didn't visit him much anymore because I was so busy with school and sports and planning for college. Grandma took care of him day and night until she was killing herself keeping him alive. Finally, he had to go to the nursing home.

I couldn't remember ever looking him in the eye and telling him I loved him. But I wanted to.

That's when I decided I wanted to visit him again.

i took his hand . . .

I drove up to the care facility without bringing my parents along. I'm still not sure why it was so important for me to go. I couldn't remember anything kind he'd ever done or said to me. But he was my grandpa, you know? Maybe I just needed to see him again before the inevitable happened. Maybe I wanted to know that my note years before hadn't made him worse.

Grandpa was a man I'd never liked, yet for as long as I could remember, I'd struggled to love him. Have you ever felt like that? It's kinda hard to explain, but I'll bet you can understand what I mean.

Somehow I had to tell him.

"You still work at that Bible camp?" he grunted, without looking over at me from his wheelchair.

"Yeah. Ah, lots of people fish in the lake," I said stupidly.

"Do you fish?"

"No, not too much."

A long uncomfortable, hesitant pause.

"Still driving that car? That—"

"Honda? Yeah. And it's paid for now."

Back and forth we talked until all of a sudden it was time to go and nothing had been said.

I stood up awkwardly. Someone came to wheel him away for supper.

But before they could, I blurted out, "Before I go, could we pray?" Without really waiting for an answer, I shut my eyes and started to pray aloud, right there in the lobby of the nursing home. It wasn't pretty. I've never been that eloquent. But I meant it. It was my first and only prayer with my grandfather.

Then I said "Amen" and I looked up.

He was crying. It might have been the stroke—he couldn't control his body much any more. Or it might have been he was trying to express something he'd never learned the words to say. I don't know.

Only one hand was still working the way he wanted it to. After our prayer it was that hand that I took when I told him I loved him.

Then I watched as they wheeled him slowly down the hall.

i don't feel guilty anymore

I don't know if he even remembered the note I wrote to him. It was never mentioned again. But I don't feel guilty about writing it any more. Telling people about God's love never makes them worse. Sometimes it makes them uneasy, sometimes it shakes them up, sometimes it even makes them angry. But they're not getting worse, they're finally on the road to getting better.

Even though we fumble through it sometimes, God spreads his love into the world both through us and despite us.

Grandpa died soon afterward. Peacefully, I guess. Grandma had been sitting with him. She stepped into the other room, he closed his eyes and slipped into a coma. Forty-five minutes later his journey was over.

I'm glad God doesn't tell us to like people, just love them. It would be way too hard to like some people. But to love them? Yeah, it's tough, but with God's help that's something I can do.

Is Grandpa in Heaven? I think so.

I think I'll see him again—not in a dark living room with the shades drawn, but just the opposite—a light-filled valley. I like to think God chose to prepare a little fishin' hole for him up there, instead of a mansion. God always did have a soft spot for fishermen.

Maybe someday he'll teach me to fish, after all.

what's the point?

"For the word of God is full of living power. It is sharper than the sharpest knife, cutting deep into our innermost thoughts and desires. It exposes us for what we really are" (Hebrews 4:12).

God's word is like a scalpel. Separating truth from lies and exposing all the diseased areas of our sinful lives. And sometimes that hurts. But once we realize who we are in God's eyes, we finally have the chance to receive God's gift of life. And be made better. Forever.

a planet full of zombies

A few years ago I saw a horror movie called *The Night of the Living Dead*. It was about these corpses that came to life because of a solar flare (or something like that). They were dead, but they moved around like living people. They didn't even know they were dead! They had no emotions, all they did was try to kill—and eat—other people. They were zombies—dead, rotting corpses that were somehow able to move. It was pretty frightening. And disgusting.

Now, imagine a whole planet of zombies. Dead people walking around, never experiencing true life, and not even realizing they're missing out.

Believe it or not, that's a pretty accurate picture of how the Bible describes people before they come to Christ:

"Once you were dead, doomed forever because of your many sins. You used to live just like the rest of the world, full of sin . . . All of us used to live that way, following the passions and desires of our evil nature" (Ephesians 2:1-3).

See? A world filled with the living dead. Pursuing evil. Doomed forever. But then God came down. Jesus lived and died and conquered death. And he offers life without end to all who believe *"no matter who we are or what we have done" (Romans 3:22).*

A stinking corpse can't *act* its way back to life. It can't *will* its way back to life. It's dead! The only way life can come is if it's somehow given to the corpse from another source. A power that's not under the control of death.

spiritual incense seven
faith in Jesus Christ alone brings new life

"But God is so rich in mercy, and he loved us so very much, that even while we were dead because of our sins, he gave us life when he raised Christ from the dead. (It is only by God's special favor that you have been saved!)" (Ephesians 2:4, 5).

A distinct change occurs in people's hearts and lives when they become Christians. It's like they're given brand-new lives. And to God, they stop smelling like dead, rotting corpses, and begin to smell like his Son, Jesus.

one way out

Most people are zombies. They go through the motions of being alive, but inside they're spiritually dead. They live without God and without hope in the world (Ephesians 2:12). And there's only one way to get off this planet alive: Faith in Jesus Christ as your Savior.

It's all about Jesus. Not religion. Not spirituality. Not tolerance. Not your own personal spirit guide. You can memorize the whole Bible, pray until you're blue in the face, hold healing services for little old ladies, talk in ancient Egyptian and eat monkey meat, but if it's not about Jesus, it's all wasted effort.

It all boils down to how you answer the question Jesus asked his followers, *"Who do you say I am?" (Mark 8:27-29).* It's the question he asked my Grandpa when he left this planet. It's the one he'll ask me. It's the one he'll ask you.

Is Jesus your Savior? Faith in Jesus Christ alone brings new life.

"For if you confess with your mouth that Jesus is Lord and believe in your heart that God raised him from the dead, you will be saved. For it is by believing in your heart that you are made right with God, and it is by confessing with your mouth that you are saved" (Romans 10:9, 10).

to review, here are the seven spiritual truths you need to know to become a Christian . . .

- Number one: You matter to God.
- Number two: God is holy and perfect.
- Number three: Sin separates people from God.
- Number four: Jesus paid the debt of your sins and rose from the dead to offer you new life.
- Number five: God offers lasting hope through Jesus Christ, no matter what you've done.
- Number six: Repentance means turning to God and letting him change the direction of your life.
- Number seven: Faith in Jesus Christ alone brings new life.

We are declared "not guilty" when we trust in Christ alone. When you admit your sin to God, he doesn't rub it in. He rubs it out. If you've never placed your trust in Jesus Christ and accepted God's gift of eternal life, do so now. Tell God that you are a sinner, that you have no hope without him. Ask him to forgive you and then place your faith, your life and your future in his hands.

You might wish to pray something like this:

Dear God, I want to be a part of your family. I want to experience that spiritual rebirth and stop living like a zombie. I admit I'm a sinner and can't get to Heaven on my own. I know that Jesus lived, died, and rose again to forgive my sins. Today, I place my trust in him and I turn my life over to you. I repent of my past and give you my future. Thanks for being my Savior, Jesus. I can't wait to smell more like you. Amen.

It's not the prayer you pray or the words you say, but rather the attitude of your heart. At the moment when you believe in Jesus Christ as your Savior, you are given new life from God. And Heaven is guaranteed. You are no longer a zombie. You can finally start on the journey toward smelling like God.

> ***"But to all who believed him and accepted him, he gave the right to become children of God. They are reborn! This is not a physical birth resulting from human passion or plan—this rebirth comes from God" (John 1:12, 13).***

A Jewish religious teacher, Nicodemus, came to speak with Jesus one night and questioned him about his teachings from God. Jesus told him, *"Unless you are born again, you can never see the Kingdom of God" (John 3:3).* Nicodemus was confused by the phrase "born again," since a man cannot return to his mother's womb. Then Jesus explained more fully, *"No one can enter the Kingdom of God without being born of water and the Spirit" (John 3:5).*

When someone trusts in Christ, he or she makes a public identification with Jesus through baptism. In Romans 6, Paul uses baptism as a metaphor for showing why we should live our lives for God. Going under the water symbolizes the burial of Christ as well as the death of our old lives. And since we have been "raised," or come up out of the water, why would we want to live in the destructive and useless ways we used to live? *"And just as Christ was raised from the dead by the glorious power of the Father, now we also may live new lives" (Romans 6:4).*

In the next section, you'll learn about living this new life for God.

learning to serve the Son

I used to live in a house where two skunks had made a den under the kitchen. Their skunky smell came up through the floorboards. It permeated that whole part of the house. And if you spent any significant amount of time in the house, you'd get the fragrance of skunk on your clothes. It was really gross.

Even after we got rid of the skunks, the smell lingered. The skunks had left their mark on that house and it took awhile to air everything out. The first thing we needed to do was get rid of the source of the nasty smell, and then we needed to replace it with something that smelled better.

If you've become a Christian, the sour smell of sin is fading. It may linger for awhile, but slowly God is fumigating your life and replacing the old smell with the aroma of Jesus. And that happens as you learn what it means to serve Jesus each day, becoming more and more like him.

In this section, you'll learn the seven keys to serving Jesus. Each one is a spiritual air freshener that will help you smell more and more like God's Son.

No matter how bad your old way of life might have smelled.

life on the edge

What happens once I become a Christian? Do I just have to obey a bunch of new rules?

From the second grade until I left home for college, I had pet turtles. Tommy. Jerry. Arnold. Spike. Lumpy. And Clyde. I always chose guy names for my turtles and then one day I found out Spike was a girl.

Oops.

They stayed in a little aquarium in my bedroom, swimming with their noses against the glass, or sitting quietly on the rocks I'd provided for them.

Eventually, they all died off except for Spike.

And then, after I left home for college, I realized I wouldn't be able to take care of Spike anymore. So one weekend when I was visiting my parents, I decided to let Spike go.

out of the aquarium

I lifted her out of her aquarium and carried her to the backyard where there was a lake.

"Goodbye Spike, you're free," I said. "Go on. Swim away. You have a whole pond to live in now!" Then, I kissed her and set her down in the water. (Yeah, I kissed my turtle. At least she was a girl.)

But then, a strange thing happened.

No, she didn't turn into a princess or anything. But she didn't swim away, either. She just sat there staring at me. She looked toward the freedom of the lake and then back at me.

"Go on, Spike. You're free now! Swim away!"

But she just stayed there. A whole lake lay before her. A new world stretched out in front of her, but she chose to stay right where I'd put her. Finally, after about 20 minutes, she ventured out a little, looked back at me, and then disappeared beneath the surface.

"Good-bye my old friend," I said, wiping tears from my eyes.

It was very emotional. A real Kodak moment. (Don't worry, I got over her.)

But as I walked back to the house, I couldn't get that image of Spike out of my mind: I'd set her free and she didn't go anywhere.

stop falling out of bed!

A few years ago a man named Bobby Brown told me a story about a guy who kept falling out of bed every night. "Do you know what his problem was?" asked Bobby.

"No," I said.

"The trouble was that he stayed too close to the place he got in."

Most Christians stay too close to the place they got in. They never venture out into the depths of what it means to truly follow God. God has set us free from aquarium life, he has opened up a whole new world for us, and yet we're afraid to leave the shore and experience the fullness and richness of life that God intended. We're afraid to start smelling like God.

Look what Jesus said he came to give his followers:

> *"My purpose is to give life in all its fullness" (John 10:10).*

Some people think Christianity is restricting, boring, lifeless, dull or limiting. But here Jesus is saying, "You got it all wrong. I came to give ultimate life. It's what I lived for. It's what I died for. That's what I offer! More freedom. More peace. More meaning. More joy than you've ever imagined. If you want to experience life to the fullest with the most possible joy, freedom, purpose and pain . . . step over here and follow me. If you want the dry juiceless existence of never really tapping into life itself, go your own way."

Jesus isn't here to limit us, but to set us free: *"So if the Son sets you free, you will indeed be free" (John 8:36).* Freedom, not restriction. That's what lies at the heart of following Jesus.

what's the point?

"For there is only one God and one Mediator who can reconcile God and people. He is the man Christ Jesus. He gave his life to purchase freedom for everyone" (1 Timothy 2:5, 6).

The last seven chapters were about getting to know God. Finding out who he is and what he desires for you and your life. Before you can even begin to smell like God, you need a relationship with him.

These next seven chapters will show you what it means to serve Jesus. Here you'll learn how to begin spreading around the fragrance of God. After you get to know God and become a believer in Christ, the adventure of following Jesus begins. It's time to leave the aquarium. The greatest experience of all lies before you.

"Since you have been raised to new life with Christ, set your sights on the realities of heaven, where Christ sits at God's right hand in the place of honor and power. Let heaven fill your thoughts. Do not think only about things down here on earth" (Colossians 3:1, 2).

so what do i do now?

What do you do now that you're a Christian? What's next? Is there something you have to do right away? Actually, there is. But it's not what you'd expect. Most churches say the first thing you need to do once you trust in Christ is to raise your hand or pray at the altar or fill out a little visitor's card or be baptized or read your Bible or join a youth group or give up smoking or stop dancing or move to Pakistan and become a missionary. And the list goes on.

And, while some of that might be good advice, it can be frustrating for new believers to hear lists like that. They end up feeling more enslaved than ever!

Here's the one thing you need to do when you become a Christian: Stop asking what you need to do now that you're a Christian.

Instead, start getting to know God more intimately. When you begin to pursue your relationship with God and look for ways to follow Christ's commands, you'll stop asking, "What do I have to do to please God?" and start asking, "What can I do to honor God?" Because you'll realize you're not under the obligations of the law, but under the freedom of grace:

"So Christ has really set us free. Now make sure that you stay free, and don't get tied up again in slavery to the law" (Galatians 5:1).

"Sin is no longer your master, for you are no longer subject to the law, which enslaves you to sin. Instead, you are free by God's grace" (Romans 6:14).

"Wherever the Spirit of the Lord is, he gives freedom" (2 Corinthians 3:17).

See that? Freedom! No more aquarium life. It's like God lifts you out of the tiny glass aquarium of your old life and sets you into a wide-open world of opportunities and the ultimate adventure of following him.

But hold on a minute. Doesn't freedom mean doing anything you want? Doesn't it mean that now you can disobey God even more?!

Well . . . yes. And . . . no.

what freedom is not

Freedom of speech doesn't allow you to publicly slander other people without consequences, or yell "Fire!" in a crowded auditorium or threaten someone's life. Even where there is freedom, there are restrictions in place to preserve and protect that freedom for everyone. And if you break the rules, there are consequences.

Imagine that your dad hands you the car keys and says, "You have my permission to drive anywhere in the country! You're free to go anywhere you want!"

Would you start by driving across the lawn, head for a swamp and then aim your car toward a 1000-foot cliff?

I doubt it. You'd naturally understand that you're free to follow the roads and obey the traffic signals and drive within the limits of the law. Your freedom is not a license to do whatever you want, but an opportunity to travel to new destinations!

The roads are there to allow you the most possible freedom, not to restrict you. The traffic laws are there to protect you so that you can drive without fear and danger. Together they provide you the opportunity to find the most possible freedom that the open road allows.

That's what following Jesus is like. That's what God's Word provides. The greatest freedom comes from obedience.

"I run in the path of your commands, for you have set my heart free" (Psalm 119:32, NIV).

We've been set free not to sit in the driveway, drive around in circles or crash at the bottom of a cliff. Instead, we can decide on a destination and take off! God's Word gives us guidelines that provide the most possible freedom, protection, purpose and direction. So that we can actually go somewhere significant. And not just sit there in the pond.

free *from* what?

From what does Jesus set us free? Well . . . regrets, worry, fear, shame, bitterness, envy, slavery to sin, death, the approval trap, pleasing people, legalism and more. God sets us free from the mistakes of the past so that we can serve him with dignity and without shame in the present.

All is forgiven. You can hold your head up high. The past is gone— with all of its baggage, guilt, shame and regrets. God has forgiven you for the wrongs you've done and will begin to heal you of the wounds you still carry.

God also frees us from our fears and worries about the future. When we're secure in the knowledge that God is in control, we have no need to fear what tomorrow will bring. No need to worry about what might go wrong. We may not know what the future holds, but we know who holds the future.

Okay, so we're free from the past and the future. So what now? What happens next? What are we set free *for*?

free *for* what?

We're set free to live as children of God, to serve him, please him and grow closer to him. To enjoy the richness of life in all its complexity and wonder. We're set free to participate in something meaningful, significant and lasting. To receive forgiveness, love and peace.

We're free to use and enjoy all the blessings that come from God. We're free to talk to God in prayer and grow closer to him through reading the Bible. We're free to worship him without shame or fear.

We're free to use our gifts, interests and abilities for God's glory and pleasure. We're free to grow in all the right directions. We're free to serve and please and honor God.

And we're free to follow Jesus down the road of life—wherever that may lead.

spiritual incense eight
serving Jesus means walking in the freedom and fullness of life

Once you become a believer, Jesus actually begins to influence your life to the point that the Bible says Jesus begins to live *in* you and *through* you. *"For this is the secret: Christ lives in you, and this is your assurance that you will share in his glory" (Colossians 1:27).*

Our assurance of Heaven is not what we do or don't do, but Christ himself living in our hearts! We don't have to worry about following a bunch of rules, we just have to follow Jesus.

"I myself no longer live, but Christ lives in me" (Galatians 2:20).

The secret to smelling like God is realizing that it's Jesus expressing himself through you that smells so good. As you hand over the reins of your life to him and say, "Take me where you want me to go!" you'll start to smell more like God every day.

If God is your copilot, switch seats! Embrace the moment. Pursue your dreams. Live without regrets. He wants you to experience all the fullness life has to offer, all the joy and peace possible. Life on the edge.

> *"But for you who fear my name, the Sun of Righteousness will rise with healing in his wings. And you will go free, leaping with joy like calves let out to pasture"* (Malachi 4:2).

Or like turtles released from the aquarium.

Life to the max. The ultimate adventure. That's what Jesus came to provide. That's what he promises. It's the journey of a lifetime and there's no turning back. Are you ready to sign on? Once you place your faith in him, the adventure has begun!

zeroes to heroes

Will God stop loving me if I mess up? What if I do something bad after becoming a Christian? Will God send me to Hell if I don't go to church or act good enough?

A Modern Retelling of Hebrews 11

What is faith? It is the confident assurance that what we hope for is going to happen. It is the evidence of things we cannot yet see. God gave his approval to ~~people~~ **teenagers** ~~in days of old~~ **today** *because of their faith.*

It was by faith that Jessica broke into tears as she thought of returning home after camp. She knew God wasn't happy with her choice of friends back home and the things she'd done with them. She wished it would be as easy to act Christian back at her high school as it was at this Christian camp where there was so much acceptance and love. She knew she needed to make a change. Though she was afraid, by faith she vowed to stay friends with God, even if it meant losing some of her other friends along the way.

It was by faith that Andy, when the doctors told him he had a rare heart disease, faced surgery and received a pacemaker even though he was only a junior in high school. After the operation, it wasn't uncommon for the pacemaker to restart his heart several times a month. Not too many teenagers wake up each morning wondering if their heart is gonna make it through the day. But Andy did. Yet, even though he questioned why this had to happen to him, he never blamed God. And he never turned his back on God despite all the uncertainty and struggles. He continued to show up at his youth group's Bible studies and he brought everything to God in prayer. And through it all, Andy trusted that God would prove faithful, even if the muscles of his heart didn't.

It was by faith that Kara refused to accept money for babysitting, even though she had no other job. She looked at sitting as her ministry of helping families in her church who didn't have enough money to pay sitters. To Kara it was no big deal. She just trusted that when she provided help for another family, God would help take care of hers.

It was by faith that Christopher said "yes" to God's call into the ministry while listening to a devotion on commitment. Even though Chris was one of the brightest high school students in Wisconsin and had been accepted into a prestigious college with a full academic scholarship, he decided that God wanted him in the ministry rather than some high-paying corporate job. Chris could have pursued a career with lots of money and prestige, but he didn't. He felt God prompting him to do something with his life that was more important than anything money could buy.

It was by faith that Katie realized she couldn't get into Heaven because of her parents' faith. Everyone thought she was a "super-Christian" because her parents happened to be missionaries. For awhile she liked the fact that everyone thought she was so close to God because it made it easier to hide that she wasn't really a believer. No one else, not even her parents and closest friends, knew she had been living a lie for years.

One day at a youth gathering, she realized that what others thought of her didn't really matter, but what God thought of her did. So she stood up in front of over 100 of her friends and said, "I'm not saved, but I want to be." She thought everyone might make fun of her for pretending that she believed in Jesus for so long, but she longed for intimacy with God more than she feared rejection by others. God honored her decision and she never regretted the day she placed her trust in him.

It was by faith that Sarah, even though she was only 13 years old and knew it had been a mistake to get pregnant, faced ridicule at her school and saw her pregnancy to term. She watched people whisper in the halls, turn their backs as she approached and shake their heads when they thought she wasn't looking. Though many of her friends and relatives encouraged her to "get it taken care of," she refused to have an abortion and eventually delivered a healthy baby boy. She knew it wasn't God's will to have sex with her boyfriend in the first place, but she trusted that making one mistake was better than making two.

How much more do I need to say? It would take too long to recount the stories of Peter, Stephen, Whitney, Stephanie, Miguel, Gretchen, Aaron or Tamika who through faith are going on mission trips to Peru, sacrificing their summers to work at Bible camps, volunteering at health clinics in Guatemala, planning children's retreats, learning to accept life-threatening illnesses in their parents, leading their friends to Christ and embracing God's plan for their lives rather than clinging to their own plans.

And there isn't space to mention the thousands of other teens who stand in unity around their flagpoles praying for their teachers, who plan Bible studies, write skits, attend prayer meetings, give to the poor, build homes for the homeless, feed the hungry and give their time to help victims of floods, earthquakes and hurricanes.

They're changing their families, churches and communities. They refuse to be intimidated, they pursue peace and reconciliation, and they stand up for their Savior every day.

Some face ridicule and rejection at their schools or jobs, others receive only insults and abuse for their beliefs. Some have been beaten, made fun of, jeered at and even tortured for their faith. Some have had loaded guns leveled at their faces and been asked if they believe in God. Others have been shot in the back as they worshiped at their church or prayed at their school. Yet through it all, they cling to a God they can not see and a promise they have not yet received. Therefore God is not ashamed to be called their God and he has prepared a city for them.

These are all commended for their faith; God has something better in store for them.

> *Therefore, since we are surrounded by such a huge crowd of witnesses to the life of faith, let us strip off every weight that slows us down, especially the sin that so easily hinders our progress. And let us run with endurance the race that God has set before us. We do this by keeping our eyes on Jesus, on whom our faith depends from start to finish" (Hebrews 12:1, 2).*

All those teens followed Jesus by faith. They kept their eyes on him, and it changed their lives. They all smelled just like God.

Serving Jesus by running the race means keeping your eyes on him and living a life of faith that reflects your new identity as a believer.

Our faith starts with Jesus and he brings it to completion. And the moment that we start believing in him, a change occurs deep in our lives. A change that will last forever.

what's the point?
i'm just not myself today!

Augustine, one of the most influential Christian thinkers and philosophers of all time, wasn't converted until he was over 30 years old.

As a young man living in fourth-century North Africa, Augustine was a hot-blooded rebel—sleeping around, partying . . . he even joined a cult.

When he returned home from Italy after being converted to Christianity in 386 A.D., he noticed an attractive lady with whom he'd spent many nights. She called out to him invitingly.

But Augustine kept walking.

"Augustine!" she called again, making clear what she was proposing. Still he didn't respond. Finally, running up to him she said, "But Augustine! It is I! It is I!"

He turned to her and replied, "Yes, I know. But it is not I."

When you trust in Christ, a change takes place in you that will affect your choices, lifestyle and attitudes. Things that didn't bother you before may now start to make you uncomfortable. Language and joking that seemed natural before may begin to sound unnatural or offensive.

Why? Because you're no longer yourself! You're a new and different person. The moment you become a Christian, God gives you an awesome new identity.

"Therefore, if anyone is in Christ, he is a new creation; the old has gone, the new has come!" (2 Corinthians 5:17, NIV).

This doesn't mean you don't care about your old friends, or that you aren't willing to spend time with them or that you're better than they are. It simply means you shouldn't be surprised when you don't "fit in" like you used to. You have a totally new identity. You've started to smell like God!

just wait 'til i hatch!

Have you ever heard Hans Christian Anderson's story of the ugly duckling? There was this beautiful swan that grew up in a pond of ducks. But when the swan was a baby, it was so ugly none of the other ducks would play with it. They rejected it, looked down on it and made fun of it. Yet as it grew, something unexpected happened. It changed. It became beautiful.

Believers are all baby swans. The world points and laughs and mocks. "Look at the Christians! Check out the Jesus freaks! You're ugly! You stink!" They yell.

Ah, but just wait.

We're growing. Becoming more like our heavenly Father. And when Christ returns everyone will see us for who we really are with our new identities, our true identities, finally revealed. Then we will be complete!

"Yes, dear friends, we are already God's children, and we can't even imagine what we will be like when Christ returns. But we do know that when he comes we will be like him, for we will see him as he really is" (1 John 3:2).

how you've changed since trusting in Christ:

- Though you were dead, you've been given new life! (Ephesians 2:5)
- Though you were excluded from God's promises, you now belong to Christ! (Ephesians 2:12, 13)
- Though you were far away from God, you've been brought near to him! (Ephesians 2:13)
- Though you were an enemy of God, you're now at peace with him! (Ephesians 2:14)
- Though you were a stranger, you're now a member of God's family! (Ephesians 2:19)

who you've become because of Christ:

- You are holy and without fault. (Ephesians 1:4)
- You have been given the Holy Sprit. (Ephesians 1:13)
- You are guaranteed Heaven. (Ephesians 1:14)
- You have a reserved seat in Heaven. (Ephesians 2:6)
- Your life is God's masterpiece. (Ephesians 2:10)
- You can go fearlessly into God's presence. (Ephesians 3:12)

the smell of death

"Our lives are a fragrance presented by Christ to God. But this fragrance is perceived differently by those being saved and by those perishing. To those who are perishing we are a fearful smell of death and doom. But to those who are being saved we are a life-giving perfume" (2 Corinthians 2:15, 16).

I know what you're probably thinking, "Hold on a minute! I thought smelling like God was a good thing! Now you pull out this verse that says we are a *'fearful smell of death and doom'*! What's that all about? I thought this Christian life was supposed to be so fulfilling, and now you tell me I'm gonna smell like a rotting corpse? What's up with that?!"

Just this. Those who reject the good news of God's love find the message of Christ repulsive. They don't want anything to do with confessing their wrongs or repenting or turning to God. They'd rather be "tolerant" of everyone's views and "open-minded" in religious matters. They're content to do things their own way. So the whole idea of humbling themselves before God and trusting in Jesus is foolishness to them and they're offended by it.

To them, we smell disgusting. They're like those ducks, pointing at baby swans. But they have no idea how beautiful we are becoming to God each day as we share the "life-giving perfume" of his grace with others.

off with the old

As a snake grows, it has to shed its old skin. If it doesn't, that old skin will fester and get infected and cause the snake to get sick. In ancient cultures, people believed that snakes live forever. They thought each time a snake shed its skin, it got a new life. Well, we've gotta shed our old skins, too.

"Since you have heard all about him and have learned the truth that is in Jesus, throw off your old evil nature and your former way of life, which is rotten through and through, full of lust and deception. Instead, there must be a spiritual renewal of your thoughts and attitudes" (Ephesians 4:21-23).

spiritual incense nine
serving Jesus means living a life of faith that expresses your new identity as a believer

We have a new identity and a new responsibility. We are called to live lives of faith and righteousness that reflect our identity as children of God. Sin is not in our interests, desires or identity. We went from lowly to holy, from zeroes to heroes. God doesn't just remodel your old life, he gives you a radical new one.

When you become a believer, the Bible says you go from death to life. And life with God is one of victory and freedom. And faith.

You can live a life of faith, too, just like those teenagers of today and those people in days of old.

So, if you don't feel like yourself any more, it may be a good thing—God is shaping you to be more—and smell more—like Jesus!

what's your nickname?

Names were important in the Bible. Jesus nicknamed Peter "the Rock" (Matthew 16:18) and James and John, "the Sons of Thunder" (Mark 3:17). The followers of Jesus nicknamed a man named Joseph "Barnabas," which means "Son of Encouragement" (Acts 4:36). Barnabas smelled like God. Acts 11:24 describes him:

"[he] was a good man, full of the Holy Spirit and strong in faith."

What would your nickname be? Maybe, "Son of Complaining," "Daughter of Gossip," "Brother of Anger," "Sister of Arguing" or "Friend of Unforgiveness"?

Or something like, "Son of Self-Control," "Daughter of Purity," "Brother of Patience," "Sister of Kindness" or "Friend of Forgiveness"?

Think of nicknames for the teens mentioned at the beginning of this chapter. Then, before going to bed tonight, choose a nickname you'd want God to give you and start living out a lifestyle that matches it!

its fangs were closing on my thumb

What should I do when I feel like doing something wrong? What if it's really tempting and I want to do it, even though I know I shouldn't? How can I follow Jesus then?

"Don't step in the water," warned Chris. "This river is swimming with cottonmouths. Just last year a seven-footer killed a cow wading downstream. It was dead and bloated by the time it reached the other shore. Be careful."

It was the twenty-first day of a month-long wilderness trip for at-risk youth. As college students, Chris, Alden and I were leading the group of ten teenagers to a secluded campsite in the Shawnee National Forest in southern Illinois.

All ten students listened intently as Chris described in detail how the cow died, writhing in pain, its throat swollen shut. Then he launched into a lecture on copperheads, another type of venomous snake found in the region. Meticulously, he explained the effects of copperhead venom on the human body. I caught myself glancing to Alden. We grinned despite his graphic descriptions. *He's just trying to scare them*, I thought, trying to downplay to myself how serious a venomous snakebite would be this far from civilization.

The students on the trip were some of the toughest and most troubled teens in Illinois. Some were in for battery, assault, delinquency, drug dealing—one guy even confessed to murder. This trip was their last chance for freedom before being sent to juvenile prison. The whole idea of the course was to teach them to make better choices and to take responsibility for their behavior.

A couple students stick out in my mind.

Dan was a 5'8", 156-pound muscle. He played football and was a high school state wrestling champion. He'd been arrested for assault and battery. (I should mention that he wasn't exactly the brightest streetlight on the block. You know what I mean . . . a few fries short of a Happy Meal. The wheel was spinning, but the hamster was dead.)

Monica was the meanest, the nastiest, get-in-your-face, rip-off-your-head, and spit-down-your-neckiest girl I'd ever met. Drugs were her thing.

We had strict behavioral guidelines on our trips, but we could tell by the fifth day that Dan and Monica were taking advantage of every opportunity to get together. More than once we had to remind them of the purpose of the course, but they only sneered and said, "You never saw us sneak off together. We're not breaking any rules! You can't prove anything!" Which was true. But we could tell they were pushing the limits.

"i thought it was a garter snake!"

After lunch, we started hiking along the river toward our campsite. The day was fresh and warm, a beautiful summery sunshine filtered through the leaves and sparkled off the water. The students were about 100 yards in front of us instructors, and we thought it was gonna be a quiet, peaceful day of hiking.

Suddenly, we heard a scream from up ahead. "Staff! Staff! We need the staff up here! There's a huge poisonous snake!"

It sounded like Dan yelling. I looked at the other two instructors and we shook our heads snickering. Chris sure had scared them!

Probably just an earthworm with a glandular problem, I thought.

"We better go check it out," said Chris.

We began to jog up the trail.

As we approached, we could see the students standing motionless in a semicircle around Dan. He was squeezing the neck of a snake between the thumb and forefinger of his right hand. With his left hand he was using a stick to hold down its tail.

It was a copperhead snake. Deadly and venomous.

"I thought it was a garter snake when I caught it!" Dan gasped.

A garter snake with fangs? I thought. *Now there's a new concept!*

"What should I do? If I drop it, it'll probably bite me!"

"That's right Dan, it will," I said, unsure what else to say. Neither of the other two staff was moving. In fact, they were both staring at me.

Nothing in wilderness guide training school had prepared us for that moment—no classes on "How to Disarm a Violent Teenage Offender Wielding a Deadly Snake in Five Easy Steps."

I knew someone had to do something.

"Listen, Dan, it looks like you have three options," I said, thinking, *Natural consequences, right? Let them make choices and take responsibility for their behavior.*

I continued, "Option number one: you can drop the snake and it'll probably bite you before you can get away. Venomous snakes can strike up to three times per second."

"I don't like option one! What's option two?" he yelled, sweat beading up on his forehead.

"Option two: you can hold the snake properly in your right hand, pick up the tail in your left hand, and turn away from the rest of the group. Then toss the head of the snake away from yourself at a 45-degree angle, at which time letting go of the tail—so the snake doesn't wrap itself around your neck and bite you in the jugular vein—thereby sending the snake 20-25 feet from yourself and the rest of the group."

Of course, I had no idea what I was talking about, I'd heard about snake-throwing from a friend.

option three . . .

Dan hesitated a little and then asked, "What's option three?"

Now, I hadn't actually thought of three options, just two. But I didn't want to look stupid, so I decided to make up something on the spot. . . . "Dan, option three is—you could hand the snake to *me* and *I* will hold the snake properly in my right hand, pick up the tail in my left hand, and turn away from the rest of the group—"

"Option three! I choose option three!" he interrupted.

Before I even realized what I was doing, I had leaned forward and picked up the snake's tail in my left hand. Then, I placed the thumb and forefinger of my right hand just below Dan's on the snake's neck.

Dan let go and leaped back and stood next to Monica, shaking. "I was never afraid of that stupid snake," he said to no one in particular, flexing his muscles, trying to look cool.

Monica snickered.

Nobody else spoke. Nobody else moved.

We all looked down at the snake.

Suddenly, I realized three things: *(1) I don't even like snakes. (2) I've never held a snake before in my life. (3) If Dan is a few fries short of a Happy Meal, I must be missing the whole burger . . .*

I straightened up and was about to turn away from the rest of the group to demonstrate the proper snake-tossing procedure when I looked up at the students. Their mouths were open. They were staring at me. Slowly, Dan raised a shaky finger, pointing at the snake.

I lowered my gaze. Since my fingers were a little lower down the snake's neck than Dan's had been, the snake had more flexibility and movement with its head. And while I'd been standing there, the copperhead snake had opened its mouth and was beginning to close its fangs on my thumb.

Well, I did not turn away from the rest of the group, toss the head of the snake away from myself at a 45-degree trajectory, blah, blah, blah, blah . . .

I took one look at that snake and I made up my own maneuver: The "Get-this-stinking-reptile-as-far-away-from-me-as-possible-in-the-next-millisecond" maneuver!

"AAAHHHH!"

I tossed that snake up into the air faster than that crocodile guy on TV could've said, "G'day, mate! This snake is about to kill me!"

The only problem was, I hadn't gotten to the turning away from the group part.

I sent that copperhead snake sailing straight into the circle of teenage delinquents.

In the slow-motion rewind of my mind, I can still see it flipping and curling and twisting through the air as I stood there thinking, *This might not be good* . . .

The snake was flying straight toward Monica's head.

Thunk!

At the last possible second it veered off course and slapped into her left shoulder. Then it bounced onto the ground, stunned. She didn't even flinch.

The snake shook his head as if to get his bearings, then slithered off into the underbrush, apparently glad to get away from those crazy humans.

Everyone looked at me, then at Monica, and then back at me. I was still shaking.

"There," I said as confidently as I could. "I'm okay . . . Dan is okay . . . Monica is okay. We're all okay," pretending like there was nothing at all unusual about throwing a deadly poisonous snake at a 16-year-old girl's face.

I turned to Dan, "Don't pick up any more snakes."

"Uh, okay, Steve."

I remember filling out the safety evaluation at the end of the course.

"Did you really throw a copperhead snake at Monica's face?" my boss asked in disbelief.

"Not intentionally," I said.

what's the point?

listening to the snake

As it turned out, the snake incident was not the most unfortunate event of the trip. On the last day, Monica was taken to the hospital with stomach pains. After a series of tests the doctors discovered that she had recently contracted gonorrhea, a disease that causes sterility in 50,000 young women each year. As shock and fear swept over her face, she admitted that she and Dan had been having sex during the wilderness trip. I wasn't there when they told Dan the news.

I wish I could tell you everything had a happy ending, but real life doesn't always turn out that way.

I still think of Dan and Monica often. I can still look down and see myself holding that copperhead, watching it close its fangs on my thumb. And when I do, I think of how many snakes we pick up every day—how many lies we listen to, how many times we flirt with temptation, never expecting to become a victim.

"Pick me up," an alluring voice whispers, "I'm harmless. Come a little closer . . . I won't hurt you." We listen to the serpent, thinking it'll be all right, just this once, believing we're never gonna get bitten. And we end up crying on a nurse's shoulder like Monica, or taking a bite of fruit like Eve.

"But, I thought it was harmless!"
"I didn't know this could happen!"
"I thought it was a garter snake when I caught it!"

We like to flirt with temptation. We try to get as close as possible without getting bit. The forbidden entices us. It lures us in.

But if you're giving in to temptation, you're not following Jesus.

For each of us, the snake has a different name: pornography, pride, greed, anger, cheating, gossip, lust, profanity . . . We all know what it's like to be drawn toward doing what we know isn't right. But there is a way out. A big part of learning to smell like God is learning to deal with temptation. God's Word gives nine specific ways to respond to the temptations that squirm into your life.

"But remember that the temptations that come into your life are no different from what others experience. And God is faithful. He will keep the temptation from becoming so strong that you can't stand up against it" (1 Corinthians 10:13).

1. pray that God will deliver you from evil

Jesus taught his disciples to pray that God would *"deliver them from the evil one" (Matthew 6:13)*. When they fell asleep in the Garden of Gethsemane, he told them to *"keep alert and pray. Otherwise temptation will overpower you. For though the spirit is willing enough, the body is weak" (Mark 14:38)*.

See? On our own we're weak. We'll get overpowered. But when we pray, we're no longer on our own. We put ourselves in touch with God's powerful Spirit. Never underestimate the power of prayer in your struggle against temptation. Take your struggles to God. And trust that he will help you.

2. remove whatever leads you into sin

Everyone has different areas of weakness. Identify what usually leads you into sin and then avoid those situations, activities or people. Avoid setting yourself up for failure. Listen to what Jesus said: *"So if your eye—even if it is your good eye—causes you to lust, gouge it out and throw it away. . . . And if your hand—even if it is your stronger hand—causes you to sin, cut it off and throw it away. It is better for you to lose one part of your body than for your whole body to be thrown into hell"* (Matthew 5:29, 30).

Today he might have put it this way, *"If surfing the Internet causes you to look at porno sites, throw out your computer. . . . If driving your car causes you to break the speed limit, give away your car. . . . If watching TV causes you to want what others have, get rid of your TV. . . . If going out with your boyfriend causes you to have sex, break up and never see him again."*

"But isn't that a little drastic?" you ask. "Just to avoid a little sin?"

Yes. It is drastic. That's the point.

Jesus took sin seriously. As we follow him, we need to be just as serious about avoiding situations that lead us into doing what we know is wrong.

3. strengthen your spiritual self-control

At a basketball camp I once attended, one of the coaches defined self-discipline as "doing what you have to do, when you have to do it, and doing it as well as you can all of the time." That's a good definition of a godly life. Check out this verse:

> *"For the grace of God that brings salvation has appeared to all men. It teaches us to say 'No' to ungodliness and worldly passions, and to live self-controlled, upright and godly lives in this present age"* (Titus 2:11, 12, NIV).

Wisdom is knowing when to say "yes" and when to say "no." Self-control is being able to do it. If you have wisdom, you'll make the right choice, if you have self-control, you'll do the right thing. That's why Solomon starts the book of Proverbs by writing, *"The purpose of these proverbs is to teach people wisdom and discipline"* (Proverbs 1:2).

In ancient times, walls around a city protected the people inside from their enemies. Without walls they were totally vulnerable to attack. So it is with us. *"A person without self-control is as defenseless as a city with broken-down walls" (Proverbs 25:28).*

Don't let your defenses down. Show wisdom and self-control by doing what you have to do, when you have to do it, and doing it as well as you can, all of the time.

4. promise yourself you won't sin

A man named Job must have struggled with lust. He made a promise to himself that he wouldn't fantasize about the girls he met. *"I made a covenant with my eyes not to look with lust upon a young woman" (Job 31:1).* Apparently it worked. God called him *"the finest man in all the earth—a man of complete integrity" (Job 2:3).*

What do you struggle with? Put a name to it, and then make yourself a promise to avoid it. Write it down, and then live it out. Today.

5. equip yourself for battle

Paul reminds us that our battle against temptation is not just a physical one, it's spiritual (see Ephesians 6:11-18). Therefore, we need to be equipped with spiritual armor: truth, righteousness, peace, faith, salvation, the Word of God and prayer. You wouldn't go into a football game without pads and a helmet. Don't go into spiritual battle unarmed and unprotected! Check out those verses and then get ready for war.

6. train like a committed athlete

When I was 20 years old I ran in a marathon. My goal was just to finish without walking. After 19 miles I couldn't feel my legs. After 22 miles I was so exhausted I could barely stand up. By the 25th mile little old ladies with walkers were passing me up on the sidewalk. But I kept going and made it 15 feet past the finish line before I collapsed.

Paul compares the Christian life to the life of an athlete (1 Corinthians 9:24-27). When you feel like giving up, you gotta focus on your goal, stay committed, keep going and train hard. No slackers allowed.

7. tell yourself the truth about the sin

Sin promises to taste delicious, but after you take a bite you discover that the aftertaste is sour. You end up with regrets, shame, confusion and hurt, only to listen to that sweet, promising voice again, "Pick me up. I'm harmless." Any time a sin seems safe, watch out!

When Jesus was tempted in the desert (see Matthew 4:1-11), he battled temptation by quoting Scripture. He used truth to conquer the subtle lies of the devil. When you're tempted, do the same. Turn to Scripture. God's Word will give you the answers, truth and ammunition to withstand temptation . . . if you're willing to apply it in your life.

8. "resist the devil, and he will flee from you" (James 4:7)

Satan speaks your language. Your very own dialect. But God promises that if you resist temptation—if you stop listening to the devil—he will leave you alone. Take God up on his promise and see what happens!

9. when all else fails, run away

Joseph managed the household of a guy named Potiphar. Even though Joseph was committed to purity, his boss's wife kept coming on to him. Finally, she cornered him and begged him to sleep with her. Instead, he ran out of the house so fast that she was left holding his shirt! (See Genesis 39:10-12.) There comes a time to run away. *Before* you go too far!

spiritual incense ten
serving Jesus means resisting temptation, even when sinning seems safe

God doesn't force us to behave when temptations come our way. He gives us a choice. A chance to follow Jesus. A chance to smell like God.

If you've listened to that enticing voice in the past and suddenly discover that some snakes of temptation have slithered into your life, throw 'em away! Leave the party, say goodnight, turn around, call for help. Don't wait for the fangs to pierce your skin.

Are there any snakes in your life that you need to throw away, right now?

how would you answer maria's question?

What does it mean to follow God "wholeheartedly?" Isn't it okay to have other things that are important in your life? How can I put God first?

Maria wiped mozzarella from her chin. "So, tell me how you got started playing basketball." It was our first date and she'd just found out I was on the college basketball team. We were both college freshmen attending a small Bible college in Minnesota.

I smiled to myself secretly thinking, *Glad you asked!* This was my big chance to impress her enough for another date.

"Well, I really got serious about basketball at the end of my freshman year in high school."

"Why was that?" she asked.

"After the season, the varsity basketball coach gathered all the varsity and J.V. players in the game room for a special meeting . . ."

"Okay, men, today I'm gonna tell you what you need to work on to improve this summer."

He started walking down the line of players. "Ryan, work on that vertical leap. You'll be dunking in no time. . . . Bobby, keep up the ball-handling. I want you starting at point guard next year. . . . Brad, hit the weights. . . ."

One by one he went, encouraging first the varsity and then the junior varsity players.

I straightened up as he approached me. What would he say? I was one of only a handful of freshmen to make the J.V. team.

The whole line of guys turned around to face me. The room was still. I heard only myself breathing as I looked up into Coach Cochran's face.

"Steve . . . you were the worst player on the junior varsity. You have a 1000 hours of practice in front of you if you ever want to be a ball player. Decide today if you expect to play basketball ever again." Then he faced the rest of the students. "Okay, you're dismissed. Have a good summer."

I managed to make it home before I cried. How could Coach do that? How could he say those things to me? How could he embarrass me like that in front of all the varsity players? I looked up to those guys. I idolized them!

That day I decided that I would play basketball again. And again. And again. Until I was so good that I'd make Coach Cochran sorry he'd ever said those words. I'd prove to him that I was a basketball player.

I turned to see Maria's reaction to this first part of my story. She looked interested but not too impressed. I decided to keep going.

"That summer I practiced three hours a day, six days a week. I kept track of every minute I spent on the court, every game I played, every shot I took. That year I started on J.V. and was one of three players moved up to varsity when we went on to win the state championship.

The next summer I practiced three hours and fifteen minutes a day, six days a week. Some days I put in over nine hours. Some days I shot over 2000 shots. Every night I slept with my basketball so I'd be holding it eight hours a day longer than my competition. I'd have the edge. As a junior, I was the first player off the bench and we won the state championship again.

By now, half the pizza was gone. Again I looked over at Maria. Was that a bored look on her face? Maybe I should change the subject.

"Would you like some more soda?" I asked.

"No thanks, Steve. Keep going. I'm interested in how this story ends."

Wow! So, I *was* getting somewhere.

"The summer before my senior year I practiced over three and a half hours, six days a week. I could make 98 out of 100 free throws and slam dunk the ball. I expected to be all-conference or all-state. Maybe earn a college scholarship. Coach named me co-captain that year."

I decided to end the story there. I left out all the stuff about us not making it to the state playoffs; about my mediocre year; about my not even starting at the end of the season.

"And the rest is history," I concluded.

Maria stared across the table at me. For a long moment no one spoke.

I was feeling pretty proud of myself. Every time I told someone that story I felt important and successful. I beamed at Maria, hoping I'd impressed her enough for another date.

"Steve, that's an amazing story."

"Thank you," I said smugly.

"Let me ask you one question."

"Shoot." I leaned back in my chair, grabbed a hunk of pizza and began to munch. Maybe she was gonna ask me out for the next date! Maybe she wanted my autograph!

"Steve, what was your god in high school?"

I almost choked on my pepperoni.

"What?" I sputtered.

"From what you've told me, the most important thing for you in high school was basketball. Your life revolved around it. I was just wondering if basketball was your god in high school."

"Well, no, I mean God was my God. I'm a Christian. I was just trying to use my gifts to the best of my ability and all that stuff. Trying to bring glory to God, you know."

I knew how to talk the game of commitment. But as I was saying those words with my mouth, I was thinking back with my heart. No one had ever asked me that question before. My coach had always said, "Make basketball your #1 priority." All the basketball camps I'd attended reinforced the same message, "Be the best you can be. . . . Give it all you've got. . . . Put out 110%."

And I'd listened. I'd been a faithful follower of their definition of success. I'd sacrificed my summers, my friendships, four years of my life in pursuit of an illusion.

I remembered back to the games we lost . . . the suicide plans I made as I cried myself to sleep the night I was told I'd no longer be starting . . . the endless, scorching summer afternoons on a deserted blacktop court, shooting shot after shot after shot . . .

I'd put in my 1000 hours. And for what? For a few trophies gathering dust in the back of my closet and a story that failed to impress a friend because she cared more about me than about my accomplishments?

What *was* my god in high school?

As I thought back, I had to admit that for the last four years I'd been worshiping a leather ball with a 21-inch circumference.

Maria's question burned in my mind long after we said good-bye. I called myself a Christian and had done so in high school. How had I lost sight of God in my high school years?

It didn't happen all at once. One day in shame I vowed to prove I was important. I forgot that God accepts and loves me as I am, not for what I do. I forgot that in God's eyes I'm worth the blood of Jesus Christ, even if I'm worthless in the eyes of my coach.

Obsessed with basketball, I forgot to seek first God's kingdom and righteousness. I sought my own glory, not God's.

What was my god in high school? My life showed it wasn't the God I claimed to serve.

But the God I serve now is a God of forgiveness and grace. And he has taken those four years of guilt away.

I wonder. How would you answer Maria's question?

what's the point?

"I am the LORD; that is my name! I will not give my glory to anyone else. I will not share my praise with carved idols" (Isaiah 42:8).

Serving Jesus means reprioritizing your life. Who's number one in your life? What is (or was) your god in high school?

It's a question that can shake you up, if you're brave enough to answer it honestly. Is your god soccer? A girlfriend or boyfriend? Grades? Success? Popularity? Work? Sex? Money? Having fun? What's number one in your life? What has first place in your heart? There is no end to the list of things we use to try and fill our hearts. And the stuff that fills your heart today is gonna fill your garage sale tomorrow.

Unless the thing that fills your heart is God himself.

If you're serious about following Jesus, you gotta be ready to put him first, in everything. *"Then he said to the crowd, 'If any of you wants to be my follower, you must put aside your selfish ambition, shoulder your cross daily, and follow me'" (Luke 9:23).*

undivided devotion

Even if you're a Christian, lots of things might be dividing your heart. Money. Greed. Fame. Pride. Lust. Fear. King David prayed for a heart totally committed to God. He wanted undivided devotion:

"Teach me your way, O LORD, and I will walk in your truth; give me an undivided heart, that I may fear your name. I will praise you, O Lord my God, with all my heart; I will glorify your name forever" (Psalm 86:11, 12, NIV).

I heard someone once say, "Show me your calendar and your checkbook and I'll show you what's important in your life." You can tell someone's priorities by looking at what he spends his time and money on. How much of your calendar and your checkbook have you given to God?

Putting God first means having an undivided heart. What would you have to give up or change in your life to do that? What TV shows? What movies? What music?

Are you willing to do it?

The problem with most people isn't that they refuse to worship God, they just refuse to give him first place in everything. They think, *An hour a week for God and 167 hours for me!* Their lives are segmented into little categories. God goes over here. Homework over here. My job over there.

But Jesus wants to permeate all of your life. And he deserves nothing less.

count the cost

One day, when large crowds were following Jesus, he turned to face them. A silence fell over the crowd. Then Jesus said:

"If you want to be my follower you must love me more than your own father and mother, wife and children, brothers and sisters—yes, more than your own life. Otherwise, you cannot be my disciple. And you cannot be my disciple if you do not carry your own cross and follow me. But don't begin until you count the cost . . . So no one can become my disciple without giving up everything for me" (Luke 14:26-28, 33).

Jesus didn't pull any punches. He laid it all out for people to see. It's as if he said, "You wanna be my follower? Then this is what it's gonna mean—I get first place. Ahead of your family, your life and your possessions. You gotta be willing to give up anything and everything that gets in the way of following me. And this disciple-life is not gonna be easy. Think about it before signing on. Make sure you're ready for the kind of commitment and sacrifice I'm talking about here."

Count the cost. Evaluate the road ahead and make an informed decision about the future. Are you willing to go wherever God leads you? Do whatever he asks of you? Smelling like God isn't easy. The Bible never claims that being a Christian is a cakewalk. Instead, God promises that Christians will face persecution, rejection, suffering, loneliness, hatred and possibly even death. Serving Jesus sometimes means going where you don't want to go.

But the rewards are . . . well, out of this world.

getting your priorities straight:

- Loving God means putting him first in your life.
- Choosing God means pursuing your relationship with him every day.
- Trusting God means taking him at his Word.
- Following God means listening to and obeying his Word.
- Serving God means living a life of compassion.

wholehearted or hole-hearted?

One day, a religious teacher asked Jesus to name God's most important commandment. And maybe you remember Jesus' response, *"Love the Lord your God with part of your heart, a little of your soul, a fraction of your mind and an ounce of your strength."*

Right?

Not quite.

"Jesus replied, 'The most important commandment is this: "Hear, O

Israel! The Lord our God is the one and only Lord. And you must love the Lord your God with all your heart, all your soul, all your mind, and all your strength""" (Mark 12:29, 30).

It's an all or nothing deal. He wants our undivided attention, devotion and commitment. He doesn't want the leftovers and he doesn't want the fringe. He wants to be at the heart of the matter. He wants to invade every corner of your life.

And when he does, you'll smell just like him.

Have you been keeping your distance from God? Holding back some parts of your life from him? If so, it's time for you to hand those areas of your life to God. He won't settle for second place. Are you willing to put him first?

spiritual incense eleven
serving Jesus means putting God first in every area of your life

It takes courage, commitment and perseverance to follow Jesus and make choices that reflect your faith. That's what worshiping God is all about—a lifestyle of obeying God and disobeying yourself (Romans 12:1, 2).

Following Jesus means taking his hand and letting him lead you through life. When the fog rolls in and you can't see where you're going, trust him. Don't look away. Don't take your eyes off him for a moment.

I saw a car once with nine "Play Rugby" bumper stickers on it. There's no mistaking what the owner of that car thinks is important in life.

What about you?

Odds are you don't have an idol in the middle of your dining room. But even though you don't bow before a stone cow or worship an oversized barbie doll, you might not be worshiping the true God. He wants first place. Nothing less. Nothing else. When you look at what matters most in your life, where does God fit in?

There are lots of things vying for your attention and allegiance, and God will never be satisfied until he has the place he deserves—first.

What place does he have? How would you answer Maria's question?

christianity's trademark

Why are some Christians such hypocrites? Shouldn't they be living dif-
ferently than the people of the world? Shouldn't they be living with more
love and less hate?

I met the most famous person in the world.

Not in a palace or a ballroom or an auditorium. Not at a convention center or in a stadium or at a political rally. I met him on a blazing summer afternoon in the inner-city of Boulder, Colorado. He was standing outside a Subway Restaurant.

I'd just ordered two 12-inch subs when he walked by the window.

At first I didn't recognize him. I just happened to glance out the window as he walked by. *Huh, what a weird-looking dude,* I thought.

I ate six inches. Twelve inches. Eighteen delicious inches of submarine sandwich. Then I carefully wiped the mayonnaise off my chin and smiled.

Only six inches left, but I was pretty full. For a moment, I wondered if I should throw it away. . . . *Naw, I'll just eat it on the train ride back home.*

As I left the restaurant, I saw him again. This time he was lean-ing over a garbage can. He moved slowly and deliberately, shuffling around, searching and scouring for something. Anything.

Still, I did not recognize this man.

His clothes hung in shreds, his face blackened with grime. Slowly he moved from one garbage can to another, from one dumpster to the next. He slid his hand into the stench and pulled out a moldy, drip-ping bun. Without a second thought he slid it into his pocket and continued his search.

That's when I realized he was searching for food.

I looked at the sandwich in my hand. *I can do a good deed and help this poor homeless man,* I thought.

"Here," I heard myself say. "Take this."

i saw him again . . .

I held the sandwich out to him. He didn't look up. He didn't even acknowledge me. Instead he just thrust out a claw-like hand and clutched the gift.

He said nothing as he shuffled away.

And still, I didn't know him; didn't recognize this filthy homeless man.

I strolled to the train station, impressed by my personal sacrifice. How kind and thoughtful I'd been! Chalk one up for me in the ol' good deeds department! Though I might be tempted to forget that man, I could always remember that little kindness I'd shown!

However.

I saw him again.

Once in a Cincinnati airport sitting by a heating vent. Once backing his way down a Wisconsin highway. Once in Tennessee, with his head hung low, holding a sign: "WILL WORK FOR FOOD." I've seen his face on commercials, on buses, on street corners, in alleys, outside high-rise apartments, in libraries, on park benches. He lives in Rwanda . . . Calcutta . . . Haiti . . . New York . . . far away . . . next door . . . down the street. His face seems to pop up everywhere I look these days.

Who is he?

His name is Jesus.

Yes, *the* Jesus.

In one of his stories, one of the last he told, Jesus explained that he would return and reward those who had reached out to the oppressed, the imprisoned and the poor. The King of the universe will recognize the deeds of compassion so easily overlooked on this earth.

"I assure you, when you did it to one of the least of these my brothers and sisters, you were doing it to me!" (Matthew 25:40).

In God's eyes, showing compassion and meeting the physical needs of those less fortunate than you is a practical way of expressing your love for Jesus. You actually serve *him* when you serve *them*.

And so he appears.

Each time wearing a different face, having a different need. Sometimes he's a starving child in an obscure country. Sometimes a homeless woman dragging a paper bag of her belongings down the street. Sometimes a grandmother sitting alone and forgotten in a nursing home. Sometimes an orphan from a war no one understands. Sometimes he's a prisoner who receives no mail. Or that kid everyone makes fun of, sitting up there in the bleachers, all alone. Sometimes his need is food, sometimes shelter, sometimes family. Always it is compassion.

Perhaps you've seen him.

Perhaps you handed him a soggy, half-eaten sandwich in front of the restaurant where you just enjoyed a meal. Or ignored him because he looked like a geek. Or turned your back and hurried on your way because of the filth or the stench or the booze on his breath. Maybe you thought as I have:

"He's not my problem. Someone else will help him."
"I'm in a hurry, I'll help the next one I see."
"Those people are dangerous. You need to keep your distance."
"What would people think if they saw me talking to him?"

And each time the words, *"when you did it to one of the least of these my brothers and sisters, you were doing it to me,"* fade softly into the static of everyday life. Jesus in the background. Excuses. Busyness. Priorities.

Leftovers.

And perhaps the most startling thing in Jesus' story was that none of the believers could remember a single time when they'd acted with the kind of compassion Jesus was talking about. They'd been living lives of selfless love and *didn't even realize it!*

brand-name believers ▬▬▬▬▬ what's the point?

We see brand names on everything from jeans to computers to pick-up trucks to shoes. Everything has a logo or trademark these days.

But what about Christianity? Is there any identifying mark or distinctive lifestyle that would cause someone to say, "There goes a believer in Jesus Christ! I can tell one a mile away!"?

According to Jesus, the answer is "Yes!"

But the trademark of Christianity isn't what you might expect. Listen to what Jesus told his followers:

> *"A new command I give you: Love one another. As I have loved you, so you must love one another. By this all men will know that you are my disciples, if you love one another" (John 13:34, 35, NIV).*

Jesus didn't say, "by this denomination," or "by this political party" or even, "by this faith," all men will know his disciples. Jesus said the trademark of Christianity is a lifestyle of *love.*

Love smells like God.

And not just any kind of love. Loving others with the same kind of love Jesus shows toward us. That's what will cause people to sit up and take notice. Because giving to others without expecting anything in return, loving the unlovable and showing compassion to people who don't deserve it is a totally different kind of love than the world has ever seen.

It can be as simple as a smile, a hug, a word of thanks, a phone call, a backrub, an encouraging e-mail. It might mean listening, spending time with someone, praying for or offering to help her through a tough time. It might mean just being there when he needs you. Compassion takes different forms. But the trademark of love is evident.

How do you make that kind of love and lifestyle your own? By pursuing your relationship with Jesus, growing in your understanding of who he is and what he has done for you, and by letting his love shine in and through your life. Following Jesus day by day. Choice by choice. Smelling like God all the while.

Giving God, and others, more than your leftovers.

love is not a feeling

Love is not that feeling you get in your gut while you're holding your girlfriend's hand. That might be nausea, but it ain't love. Love is not that queasy, exciting little thrill you get whenever you see her. That might be constipation, but it ain't love. Love is not a feeling, it's a *choice*. It's a decision to meet the needs of another person by serving his or her best interests despite the price, whatever the cost—and expecting nothing in return.

Love is a response. That's why God says he will lavish his love on *"those who love me and obey my commands" (Deuteronomy 5:10).* If love was a feeling he would have said, "those who love me and feel mushy about my commandments."

And love always has a genuine concern for the other person's best interest. It's not like giving away your leftovers and patting yourself on the back: *"If I gave everything I have to the poor and even sacrificed my body, I could boast about it; but if I didn't love others, I would be of no value whatsoever" (1 Corinthians 13:3).*

Love doesn't judge others based on mere appearances. In God's eyes we're all equals. *"There is no longer Jew or Gentile, slave or free, male or female. For you are all Christians—you are one in Christ Jesus" (Galatians 3:28).*

Today we might say it this way, *"There is no longer Jock or Geek, cheerleader or computer nerd, guy or girl. For you are all Christians—you are one in Christ Jesus."*

Christians sometimes make the mistake of thinking lonely people only need God. Very often, lonely people need us.

portraits of love

There is a story about a priest who painted a picture of Christ. He was very proud of the picture and wanted other people to notice it as well. So, he invited the famous author Leo Tolstoy to come over. The priest thought that if Tolstoy liked his painting, then the other priests would admire it as well. Tolstoy came into the room and sat in front of the painting. For an hour he just sat there and stared at it. The priest was getting really excited.

Then, as Tolstoy stood up to leave, the priest asked, "So, what do you think?"

And Tolstoy looked at him and said, "If you would have loved him more, you would have painted him better."

God doesn't want us to do stuff for him because we're gonna get rewarded or praised or famous for doing it. Instead, he wants our *love* for him to motivate us to do great things for him.

Don't let Jesus say to you one day, "If you would have loved me more, you would have served me better."

"But if anyone has enough money to live well and sees a brother or sister in need and refuses to help—how can God's love be in that person? Dear children, let us stop just saying we love each other; let us really show it by our actions" (1 John 3:17, 18).

Every day Christians have the chance to paint a portrait with our lives. To smell like God or stink like the world. Which will it be for you?

spiritual incense twelve
serving Jesus means living a life of love and compassion

It has always been the way of the Savior to appear where people least expect him: Back at the temple after his parents had gone . . . walking on the water in the middle of the night . . . partying with crooks and whores . . . crying helplessly in a stable . . . dying hopelessly on a cross . . . searching through a dumpster in Boulder, Colorado . . . walking alone through the hallways of your school.

He'll show up soon in your life. Keep an eye out for him.

And the next time you see him, don't just hand him your leftovers and walk away like I did. Dare to enter his world, carry his burden, share his need. Show you care.

And one day, the King himself will thank you for your kindness.

the toe-jam principle

How does God want me to live? Does being "holy" mean I have to shave my head, give up meat, marry a girl who doesn't kiss, move to Peru and eat bark for the rest of my life?

Recently, I stopped at a restaurant for lunch. As my server handed me my menu, I noticed her scratched nametag. It read: "32 YEARS OF SERVICE."

"Thirty-two years?" I blurted. "At the same restaurant!?"

"Yup," she said.

Thirty-two years?!

"That's a long time!"

"It's almost 33. It'll be 33 years on August 18th," she said.

I couldn't believe it! It was a career. A lifetime! I couldn't imagine serving in the same restaurant, waiting on people, for 32 years of my life.

I started thinking about how many years I'd been a Christian. How many of those would God consider "years of service"? How many would he consider "years of slacking"? What would my nametag read?

What about yours?

Most Christians are pretty content to just show up. To go to church. To pray. To read their Bibles and then just head back home. They pop in, feast on spiritual food, and then take off.

But there's a big difference between eating at the restaurant and actually *serving* the customers.

And Jesus calls us to serve.

check into the game

Christianity is not a spectator sport. We need to actually check into the game. We've been set free to serve, not just sit on the bench. You gotta suit up and you gotta break into a sweat.

Imagine a sport where your coach didn't care if you came to practices or not. "Show up when you want. You don't need to be committed to the team. And there are no training rules. You can party as much as you want, stay up late on the nights before games and flunk all your classes."

What would you think of a coach like that? Would you respect him? Would you value that sport very much?

Probably not.

We already know that to be a member of a team takes commitment, dedication, sacrifice and hard work. Following Christ does too!

"All those who want to be my disciples must come and follow me, because my servants must be where I am. And if they follow me, the Father will honor them" (John 12:26).

What's big enough to give your life to? What's important enough to live for? To die for?

Jesus.

And he wants you to pour your life into something that will really matter and make a lasting difference—service.

the toe-jam principle

On the night Jesus was betrayed, he went around washing the feet of his followers. You've probably heard the story. You can read it for yourself in John 13:1-17.

Jesus knew that he was about to die and he wanted to leave his followers with a powerful image of what their lives were to be like from then on. So he did what a servant or slave might have done. He knelt down and washed the feet of his friends.

And when he was done, he explained:

"And since I, the Lord and Teacher, have washed your feet, you ought to wash each other's feet. I have given you an example to follow. Do as I have done to you. How true it is that a servant is not greater than the master. Nor are messengers more important than the one who sends them. You know these things—now do them! That is the path of blessing" (John 13:14-17).

Did you catch that? Jesus said serving others—washing their feet—blesses you. That is the path of blessing. Serving others brings you good things from God. Another time Jesus put it like this: *"It is more blessed to give than to receive" (Acts 20:35).* Blessing through service. That's the Toe-Jam Principle.

It's not just knowing what to do or wanting to be helpful. It's actually *doing* it. Serving others requires action, not just head knowledge.

And serving others, just like washing someone else's feet, isn't always easy or fun. But according to Jesus, it's the pathway of blessing. It takes genuine humility to serve like that.

When Jesus introduced his friends to the Toe-Jam Principle, he gave away a secret that would change the world and unleash God's blessings in the lives of believers. Are you in on it? Once you start living the Toe-Jam Principle, life will never be the same again. Serving others blesses you. Maximum blessing comes from heartfelt service.

There was a lady who lived out the Toe-Jam Principle even before Jesus introduced it. I'd like you to meet her. Her name was Mary.

she smelled like Jesus

Every time you hear about this particular Mary she was trying to get close to Jesus. Once, as her sister fussed around the house, Mary sat at Jesus' feet. When Jesus visited after her brother Lazarus died, she dropped to her knees before him and wept. Even after Jesus died, she was in the first group of people to go to see his body.

She just couldn't get enough of being close to Jesus.

A few days before Jesus washed the disciples' feet, Mary washed Jesus' feet.

Everyone was sitting down for dinner when she walked into the room. Martha was serving the food, like always. Lazarus (whom Jesus had raised from the dead) was seated at the table with Jesus and his other buddies. And then Mary came in.

She was carrying a jar of expensive perfume. She'd probably bought it when Lazarus died a few months earlier and hadn't needed to use it. But now, she silently walked in and poured the perfume on Jesus' head and on his feet. Then, she took the perfume and, *"anointed Jesus' feet with it and wiped his feet with her hair. And the house was filled with fragrance"* (John 12:3).

In those days it wasn't socially acceptable for a woman to unbraid her hair in the presence of men. But she did it to clean Jesus' feet. Not only that, but the disciples got into a fuss about how pouring out the perfume was a waste; how if only they could have sold the perfume they could have given the money to the poor . . .

But they missed the whole point! Of course it's good to feed the poor, but she wasn't being wasteful, she was offering the best that she had to Jesus. And she didn't care what anyone thought. Nothing was gonna stop her from showing her love and devotion to Jesus. Even if it cost her everything!

And Jesus was honored by it. He said it was an act of devotion that would be whispered through the ages, whenever people told the gospel story.

And Mary didn't say a word.

She didn't defend herself to her accusers. She didn't explain herself. She didn't make a big deal out of it. All she did was bring her best to Jesus. Because she loved him.

And when she left that day, she smelled just like Jesus did.

Mary served with humility. All she desired was to be close to Jesus.

Let's take a quick look at one other biblical servant, who lived long before either Jesus or Mary.

turn off your face, dude!

At least 39 times in the Bible, Moses is referred to as "the servant of the Lord." Once God got ahold of him, he was uncompromising in standing up for God. He confronted the most powerful ruler in the world, led God's people through the wilderness for 40 years and wrote the first five books of the Bible.

Moses wanted to be close to God. To actually see him face-to-face. When he received the Ten Commandments he spent 40 days in close contact with God. And when he came down from the mountain, Moses's face actually glowed. He had to wear a veil over his face so the people wouldn't freak out! (Exodus 34:28-35).

"That old system of law etched in stone led to death, yet it began with such glory that the people of Israel could not bear to look at Moses' face. For his face shone with the glory of God, even though the brightness was already fading away" (2 Corinthians 3:7).

The closer we are to God—like Mary or Moses—the more we'll smell like Jesus. The more we'll glow in this darkened world. The secret to smelling like God and serving like Jesus is to stay intimate with God and let the Holy Spirit direct your life.

what's the point?
it fits like a glove

All by itself, a glove can't do much. It has no power to move, no ability to do anything but sit there gathering dust. It's a useless piece of cloth or leather.

But, slip a hand inside, and the glove comes to life. Now it can grasp things, pick up objects, open a door, drive a car, wiggle, wave and squirm.

"Now, wait a minute," you say, "the glove still isn't alive. It's just powered by another source, a source which has the ability to do those things. The glove is still just a glove!"

Exactly.

On our own, without the Holy Spirit, we're spiritually dead. We're lifeless. We can't do anything to please God or serve him. But, once we trust in Christ and the Holy Spirit comes to dwell within our hearts, we're made alive. The Holy Spirit empowers us and gives us both the strength and the will to live godly lives:

"Now glory be to God! By his mighty power at work within us, he is able to accomplish infinitely more than we would ever dare to ask or hope" (Ephesians 3:20).

We're finally able to do things that would have been impossible before. Like what? Well, for starters—obeying God, desiring his will above our own, humbling ourselves before him, following Christ, serving others, smelling like God.

And when we do, God will accomplish more than we could ever dream.

others may, but you cannot

When I first started working at Camp Phillip, a Bible camp in Wisconsin, the camp director gave me a sheet of paper entitled "Others May, But You Cannot." It was written by George Douglass Watson around the year 1900, and was given to my director when he left the seminary to become a pastor. Part of the letter goes like this:

If God has called you to be really like Jesus, He will draw you into a life of crucifixion and humility, and put upon you such demands of obedience that you will not be able to follow other people or measure yourself by other Christians, and in many ways He will seem to let other good people do things which He will not let you do. . . .

The Lord may let others be honored and put forward, and keep you in hidden obscurity, because He wants to produce some choice, fragrant fruit for His coming glory, which can only be produced in the shade. He may let others do work for Him and get the credit for it, but He will make you work and toil on without knowing how much you are doing; and then to make your work still more precious, He may let others get the credit for the work which you have done, and thus make your reward ten times greater when Jesus comes.

The Holy Spirit gives us each different gifts and talents. And it's our job to use them faithfully so that God's love flows through us and into the world: *"God has given gifts to each of you from his great variety of spiritual gifts. Manage them well so that God's generosity can flow through you" (1 Peter 4:10).* Look for opportunities to serve others at your home, church, school, job or in your community.

The day you decide to serve Jesus wholeheartedly, regardless of who gets the credit, is the day the fragrance of your life changes forever.

spiritual incense thirteen
serving Jesus means humbly meeting the needs of others

When you get to Heaven, what's your nametag gonna say?

God wants servants who will get down and dirty and do the jobs no one else wants. Who will tune into him and let him call the shots for their lives. With the humility of Mary and the boldness of Moses.

We think God is on a talent search for well-qualified, experienced, candidates. He's not. God doesn't call the equipped, he equips the called. He is looking for humble, bold, available and sold-out servants.

"So, my dear brothers and sisters, be strong and steady, always enthusiastic about the Lord's work, for you know that nothing you do for the Lord is ever useless" (1 Corinthians 15:58).

Are you ready to put God's agenda above your own? Are you ready to use your interests, talents, abilities and gifts to honor God? Then stop making a splash and start making a difference. Stop projecting an image, and start producing an impact. And you'll start to smell just like Moses, the servant of God. And Mary, the friend of Jesus.

one long semester in joe's porno pit

Is there anything God can't stand? What are some of the things that God really hates? What makes God sick?

"You're gonna like your roommate," said Charles, as he led me down the maze of hallways to my dorm room. "Even though he is a little . . . um . . . different."

"What do you mean Joe is different?" I asked.

Charles was the Resident Assistant (R.A.) in charge of the students in this part of the building. This was my first day on campus and I'd never been in a resident hall at a public university before. My eyes flickered across the posters on each door that we passed.

"Oh, you'll like him. Don't worry," he answered vaguely. "Well, here we are."

Charles pointed to a colorfully decorated door in front of us. Big letters across the top of it announced: *JOE'S PORNO PIT. ENTER IF YOU DARE.*

Underneath the sign, Joe had posted an article about the recent breakup of a pornography ring in his hometown, as well as several pictures I'd rather not describe.

i stepped inside

We could hear the garbled pound of rock music in the room. Charles knocked on the door. No one answered. It sounded like someone was shuffling around, closing cupboards or putting something away. Charles turned the knob and pressed open the door, "Joe?"

"C'mon in," someone grunted.

Charles motioned for me to enter and I stepped into the room.

It took my eyes a moment to adjust to the dim light. A couple of tinted lamps gave the room an eerie reddish glow. Covering the walls were posters of the 1970s rock groups KISS, Alice Cooper, Ozzy Ozborne and Led Zeppelin. A small refrigerator was nestled between the armchair and the bunk beds. On a trunk in front of me lay a pile of *Hustler* magazines. Beyond the trunk sat a figure, slumped in the armchair, staring at us. A cigarette tipped out of his mouth.

Joe reached over to the stereo on his desk and turned down the volume, then offered me his hand. "You must be my new roommate."

"Yeah, nice to meet you Joe," I said. In the gloomy darkness I fumbled for his hand and shook it.

"Well, I'll let you two get to know each other," said Charles. "Steve, if you need anything, I'm in room 113 just down the hall. I'm sure it's gonna be a great semester!"

Then he closed the door slowly behind him. As the sound of his footsteps faded down the hall, Joe turned to me.

"So, you want a beer?"

He flipped open the door to the small fridge. It was packed with bottles of beer.

"Um, no thanks," I sputtered. "I need to get my stuff moved in." I was under the legal drinking age. Joe was, too.

"Suit yourself." Joe reached in and helped himself to an already-opened bottle of beer. "I thought for sure Charles was gonna bust me when he opened that door."

"make yourself at home!"

Joe puffed on his cigarette and took a deep swig from the bottle. Even if the overhead light had been turned on and the shades hadn't been drawn, I think the room would still have seemed dark.

I didn't know what to say. I decided to just go and get my luggage. This was not at all what I'd imagined it would be like at a public university. Sure, I knew it would be different from the small Bible college in rural Minnesota where I'd spent the last year and a half, but I had no idea it would be *this* different.

All of the essentials are within reach of Joe's armchair—the porno magazines, the ashtray, the stereo, the TV, the beer. He never needs to get up for anything! I thought.

When I came back in, Joe was getting ready to leave. "Hey, you can look through my magazines. Listen to the music. Whatever. Help yourself to anything in the fridge. I'm gonna go meet some friends. There's a party tonight. I might not be back till morning, so I'll probably see you tomorrow."

"Okay, sure."

"Make yourself at home," Joe said. Then he walked out the door.

I hardly saw him all week. He spent six out of the first seven nights sleeping over at his girlfriend's apartment. I called up my friend Matt at the Bible college. "You aren't gonna believe what it's like here," I said.

"Oh, yeah? What's it like?"

"Well, my roommate smokes, drinks, listens to satanic music, reads pornography and in the first week of the semester, he only spent one night sleeping in the room."

"You're kidding! Where was he the other nights?"

"Over at his girlfriend's. Joe never studies, skips class and just mooches money off his parents."

"Whoa."

"Yeah. You're tellin' me. And I gotta live with this guy!"

Halfway through the semester I complained to Charles about the smoking and got transferred to another room. "I distinctly remember signing up for a non-smoking roommate." I said. I didn't tell Charles about the drinking or anything, and Joe got to spend the rest of the year without a roommate.

And so I left Joe's porno pit and moved my stuff down the hall.

Each week I'd see Joe walking down the hall toward his room holding hands with a different girl and I'd think to myself, *I know what they're going in there to do.* He'd usually wave to me or smile or say, "How do you like your new roommate?"

And I'd nod stiffly at him and then slip into my new room and plop down to read my Bible or do my homework.

I couldn't believe how different Joe and I were.

what makes God sick

I never saw Joe after that year. I don't know what ever happened to him. And for a long time I told people about what a shock it was to go from a Christian college to a secular university. I told them all about Joe.

But then, not too long ago, as I was telling the story again, I realized that the real story wasn't about Joe at all.

It was about me.

Now, I'm not excusing any of Joe's habits or making light of his choices. But he didn't know God and he literally couldn't help what he was doing. Paul, wrote, *"For the sinful nature is always hostile to God. It never did obey God's laws, and it never will. That's why those who are still under the control of their sinful nature can never please God" (Romans 8:7, 8).*

If I ever met a guy controlled by the sinful nature, it was Joe. He couldn't have pleased God even if he wanted to. It was against his nature.

But, you see, I knew all about God when I met up with Joe. Anyone could tell by his lifestyle that he wasn't a Christian. Yet I never took the time to share with him what I believed.

"I know all the things you do, that you are neither hot nor cold. I wish you were one or the other! But since you are like lukewarm water, I will spit you out of my mouth!" (Revelation 3:15, 16).

Let me ask you a question. Based on what Jesus said in the verse above, who would God be ready to spit out: Joe or me? A guy in total rebellion, or a wishy-washy guy who was more content to bail out than stand up for righteousness?

There's one thing God hates more than sin—people who don't care. Pretenders. Those who claim to be his followers but have no conviction to stand up for him in the world. Those who are quick to find fault with others, without ever taking inventory of their own priorities and lives. Those who act religious, but don't commit themselves to their beliefs.

People like me. And you.

We're all lukewarm sometimes. But what happens when you realize that part of your life has lost its fire for God? Do you sit by and do nothing about it? Or do you ignite the fire through worship, prayer and Bible study?

Most people live mediocre lives. They're lukewarm in everything they do. Yet, no one lacking passion has ever been great in God's kingdom. The people who accomplish great things for God always have: (1) unshakable confidence, (2) unquenchable passion, (3) whole-hearted devotion, (4) genuine humility and a (5) generous heart.

And, according to this verse, God would rather we fight against him than get in the way. God would rather we blaspheme him than ignore him. He would rather we rage in hatred against him than only *pretend* that we love him.

I started thinking that if Jesus had stepped onto our campus, Joe was the kind of guy he would have become best friends with. He would have asked to transfer into Joe's porno pit and he would have probably stayed clear of me sitting in my room reading my Bible to myself, shaking my head at what a sinner Joe was.

what's the point?

get your "but!" out of the way

There is one word you're not allowed to say to God.

It isn't a dirty word or a four-letter word. It isn't even profanity. It's a seemingly innocent little, three-letter word that God will never let his children use.

It's the first word we say when we sin. It's the word that precedes every excuse. It's that little word "but":

*"I'm sorry God, **but** . . ."*
*"I'd love to give more money to church, **but** . . ."*
*"I'd really like to help lead the singing on the youth retreat, **but** . . ."*
*"I'd stay here and tell Joe about you, **but** . . ."*

We never honor God by making excuses. And as we go into the world to spread the smell of God, we need to be bold and unashamed of God's message. We need to live lives of passion for God. On fire for him.

God hates complacency. So get your "but" out of the way.

No matter what you do or have done, God will always accept you. But he will *never* accept your excuses. Learn to say "yes!" to him. Whatever the cost. Whatever it takes. Wherever it leads.

God doesn't look for accomplishments, but faithfulness. He doesn't care how many church services you've attended, how many Bible verses you've memorized, how many things you've checked off your to-do list. What he is wondering, and what he will ask you one day, is: "Where was your heart? What was your desire? How did you live out my love for the world to see?"

no cowards in heaven

When you get to Heaven God isn't gonna ask you if you won any great battles for him here on earth. But he is gonna ask if you fought on his side.

Everyone in Heaven had to stand up for Jesus here on earth.

"If anyone acknowledges me publicly here on earth, I will openly acknowledge that person before my Father in heaven. But if anyone denies me here on earth, I will deny that person before my Father in heaven" (Matthew 10:32, 33).

It takes courage to smell like God. To show backbone. To stand up for what's right. Sometimes you gotta go against the flow. And sometimes you gotta do it in shark-infested waters. But don't back down. Stay on course. And be bold.

How bold do you have to be to go to Heaven? That's easy: Bold enough to confess your faith in Jesus and stand up for him. Check this verse out. Read it carefully and think about the different groups of condemned people God lists: *"But cowards who turn away from me, and unbelievers, and the corrupt, and murderers, and the immoral, and those who practice witchcraft, and idol worshipers, and all liars—their doom is in the lake that burns with fire and sulfur. This is the second death" (Revelation 21:8).*

In God's address book of who will be in Hell, the first people he lists are cowards. Why? Why would God punish cowards? Because it takes guts to follow Jesus and place your faith in him. And it takes guts to be on fire for God in a cold and thankless world.

How is your flame? If you've let your love for God grow cool, it's time to fan it back into flame and get rid of anything that's lukewarm in your commitment to following Christ. Make no excuses, accept none. God wants courage, commitment and wholehearted devotion in the hearts of his children.

spiritual incense fourteen
serving Jesus means boldly standing up for God with passion, love and commitment

There are few things worth dying for. There are even fewer worth living for. The question is not so much, "Are you willing to die for Jesus?" but, "Are you willing to *live* for him?"

Serving Jesus is all about making choices every day. Every moment. Every hour. Both when no one is looking, and when everyone is staring your way. In front of your friends. Your family. And people like Joe.

When people are using Jesus' name as a cuss word, say something. When your friends are mocking Christ, stand up for your Savior. When someone asks you why you go to church, tell him. When people sneer at you, don't back down. It's not easy.

But it's always worth it.

Take a bold stand for Jesus. Nothing that's lukewarm ever smells like God.

to review, here are the seven spiritual truths that will mark your life as a follower of Jesus Christ. serving Jesus means . . .

- Number one: Walking in the freedom and fullness of life.
- Number two: Living a life of faith that expresses your new identity as a believer.
- Number three: Resisting temptation, even when sinning seems safe.
- Number four: Putting God first in every area of your life.
- Number five: Living a life of love and compassion.
- Number six: Humbly meeting the needs of others.
- Number seven: Boldly standing up for God with passion, love and commitment.

Jesus, this life of following you isn't gonna be easy, but I want to walk with you all the way. Even when I'm tempted to back down or turn around, give me courage. Let me be bold and compassionate. Invade me. Change me from the inside, out. Make me your own, Lord. Fill me with your unpredictable, unstoppable, unquenchable Spirit. Blow through my life and fill me with your power and love. I want to live for you and follow you. Forever. Amen.

living to honor the Spirit

Ever notice how you don't smell your own bad breath, but you can always tell when someone else needs a breath mint? It's because you're so used to the smell of your own breath that your brain just stops processing that information. Your breath stinks, but you don't even notice!

It's the same with our lives. We're quick to point out what stinks in someone else's life, but most of the time we don't even notice the problems in our own. We tune them out.

Well, if you're serious about living to honor the Holy Spirit, then it's time to start smelling your own life. God's Spirit lives in us to comfort us with the news of forgiveness and new life, to reveal truth, to convict us of our sins and to strengthen us in our daily lives.

Every time God's Spirit points out how to apply God's Word in your life it's like a spiritual breath mint that helps you cleanse and refresh your lifestyle.

Honoring God with your life takes guts. Because when you look closely at your lifestyle choices, you might find some that really stink.

So, as you read this section, let God's Spirit point out the problem areas of your life. And then pop the truth into your heart, and apply it to your life as a spiritual breath mint that everyone (including you) will notice.

some things are not what they seem

I'm a pretty good person and I try to live a good Christian life. That must count for something, right? Isn't being good what Christianity is all about?

Some things are not what they seem.

When I first began working at Camp Phillip as the program director, I moved into an old farmhouse that a guy named Ernie had lived in. Ernie and his family had owned the farm for over 100 years and there were dozens of old sheds and barns scattered across the property.

It was early December when I moved in, and since it was winter in Wisconsin, the ground was frozen solid and covered with snow.

"You can have the cat," said Ernie, pointing to a cute little gray and white cat skittering between the barns. "She's been living here for three years. She comes with the farm."

"What's her name?" I asked.

"Pee Wee," he told me as he ducked his head into the car and drove away.

I nodded, thinking, *Okay. Ernie the Farmer and his sidekick, Pee Wee the Cat. Whatever . . .*

Then, Ernie was gone and I was in the farmhouse all by myself.

the discovery

For the first couple weeks, Pee Wee kept her distance. She'd sit and watch me from her perch near the milking barn. But she never came close enough for me to pet her. I thought maybe she was afraid of me since I was a new face and everything. I set food and water out on the porch for her, but whenever I approached, she would run off. It was kind of a one-sided relationship.

I was really busy the first few weeks unpacking my things and getting settled, so it wasn't until about a month after moving in that I decided to investigate the barns and sheds, just to see what kind of stuff Ernie had left behind.

I slipped on my winter coat and headed outside.

It was a clear crisp winter day. High, bright, blue sky above. Hard, white, frozen ground below. I could see my breath curling away from me as I stepped into the first shed.

Ernie had used this shed to hold corn, but most of it was gone now. The shed was wooden, with slits between the boards that let sunlight in, cutting long streaks of light across the hay and the corn husks left scattered on the ground.

But there was something else in the shed.

Near the far end of the shed I saw Pee Wee laying on the hay.

Maybe this is my big chance to finally pet her!

"Hey, Pee Wee!" I called. "C'mere! Pee Wee!"

But Pee Wee didn't move.

"C'mere, Pee Wee!" This time I stepped forward and stretched out my hand. Still, Pee Wee lay there, unmoving.

She must be sleeping. I'll just go wake her up.

I walked across the hay, calling gently to her. I leaned down to pet her, and then drew my hand back in horror.

She was stone-cold. Frozen.

There was no waking up this cat.

Oh, no! I picked her frozen little body up and her feet poked straight in the air. *Whoa. She's been here for awhile. No wonder she hasn't been eating very well.*

She was frozen so stiff I could hold her up by the tail.

A frozen cat-cicle.

Hm. I had a problem. I'd only been in charge of caring for this cat for a couple of weeks and I'd already murdered her.

I wasn't sure exactly what to do. What is Ernie gonna think?

I decided Ernie didn't have to know. Pee Wee was dead and I had to find a place to get rid of the body so that if Ernie returned to say "hi" he wouldn't find out. But how could I bury this cat? The ground was frozen solid! I thought about putting her in my freezer until spring, but my freezer wasn't big enough . . .

The camp freezer! Yeah! Now, that's big enough! I could just store Pee Wee in there until the ground thawed. . . . Wait a minute . . . Naw. What if the camp cooks found her? We'd be eating catburgers for weeks.

Finally, I decided to take my chances digging her a little grave out there between the sheds. I'd hold my own private cat funeral out on the farm.

I set Pee Wee down on the hay and went to the garage for a shovel. "Stay here," I told her.

She did.

the ceremony

A few minutes later I returned with a shovel and carried her body to a nice little clearing between two sheds. It looked like a good cat burial area.

I tossed the corpse into the snow and began to dig.

The ground was frozen as solid as Pee Wee.

I chipped away at the frozen soil inch by inch until, an hour later, I'd finally dug her grave.

"Whew, I hope that's big enough for you," I told her.

I set her tail-first into the hole.

Yikes. The hole wasn't even close to big enough.

Her head and two front paws stuck straight up out of the ground.

Hm. I thought, *Maybe I could take her inside and thaw her out. You know, put her in the microwave and set it at defrost. Or just leave her in the living room for a couple of hours . . .*

Naw. Since I'd already spent half of the afternoon with this cat, I decided on a more efficient, time-saving procedure.

I raised the shovel high into the air, and brought the blade down on the cat's neck.

It just glanced off her.

"Let's try this again, Pee Wee." I said aloud.

Raise shovel high. Bring it down. Crunch the cat.

Kajing!

Ah, that time it worked. Part of the frozen Pee Wee broke off and I was able to smunch her into the hole.

I shoveled the frozen chunks of dirt around her, but that's when I realized I hadn't quite scrunched her enough. The top of her head still stuck out of the ground.

I used the flat head of the shovel this time.

Whack! Whack! Whack!

Hm. This wasn't going exactly as I'd planned. The hole was still too small.

What could I do? I did the only thing I could think of. I jumped up and brought 200 pounds of pizza-fed program director down on the gray lump of fur sticking out of the ground.

A few more jumps did it. That cat was underground.

I tossed some snow on her, said my last farewell, carried the shovel back to the porch, and took the cat food inside.

the return of pee wee

I have to admit, I felt a little bad about the whole thing. First, killing a cat that had survived fine without me for three years. Then, maiming her to try and fit her into her grave. And the whole jumping-on-her-head thing. But what could I do? She was dead. She didn't know the difference.

Finally, I went back outside to look around at the other sheds.

The first one was full of wood for the stove in my basement. Good. I'd be needing that later in the winter.

I opened up the door to the adjoining shed and peered inside.

That's when I heard it.

Meow.

My blood froze in my veins. I stopped cold in my tracks.

Meow. Meow.

I turned slowly and scanned the shadows of the barn. Nothing. No one.

Naw. It couldn't be, Steve! It had to be your imagination. It's just guilt-induced fear. You've been watching too many scary movies.

This was Ernie's old tool shed. I caught myself looking at the hammers and crowbars hanging from the shelves wondering how well they would work as weapons.

And then I heard it again. This time closer.

Meow. Meow.

My heart was hammering. *It can't be! You were dead! I just buried you in the cold frozen ground! I chopped you with a shovel! I jumped on your head!*

Slowly, I turned and looked toward the entrance of the shed. There she stood. Pee Wee the Cat. Alive and well. Same gray and white markings. Same soft fluffy tail.

No! There is no way! You were a frozen chunk of meat a few minutes ago! She's come back to haunt me! I'm a cat-killer being stalked by the ghosts of my past!

She bounded up onto the wood pile, turned and looked at me and then disappeared behind the stack of logs.

I bolted out of the shed and ran to the place I'd buried Pee Wee. I had to see for myself. I had to be sure.

When I got to the grave, I kicked the chunks of snow to the side and, sure enough, there was Pee Wee's frozen, furry little head sticking out. One lifeless eyeball stared unblinkingly at the harsh winter sun.

Whew! What a relief!

I looked back toward the tool shed. And there stood Pee Wee's twin.

There were two of them! This whole time! Ernie never said there were two of them! Two cats! Huh! I wasn't scared for a minute!

I renamed the living cat, "Ghost," and we became good pals. For the next four years Ghost stayed there at the farm. For all I know she's still there.

And as for Pee Wee, the frozen cat, well . . . I *know* where she is. Back between the corn sheds. Resting in peace. Or . . . I should say, pieces.

Some things are not what they seem.

I thought the cat was asleep, but she was dead. I thought there was only one cat, but there were two. I thought I could dig her a big enough grave, but the ground was too frozen. And then, when I heard her meowing, I didn't know what to think! Appearances can be deceiving!

There are lots of things in life that aren't what they first appear to be. People deceive us. Promises are broken. Masks hide the real motives. Only when the light of truth shines in can you see clearly how messed up your first impressions were.

In the same way serving Jesus, honoring the Holy Spirit and smelling like God are not what they appear to be.

"He saved us, not because of the good things we did, but because of his mercy. He washed away our sins and gave us a new life through the Holy Spirit" (Titus 3:5).

part of the family

what's the point?

Most people think being a Christian is all about going to church, being good, following the rules and doing your best. You ask someone, "Are you a Christian?" and you hear:

"Oh, I try to live a good Christian life."
"Well, I hope so."
"I go to church."
"I like to think of myself as a Christian."
"I was baptized."
"I'm not as good a person as I'd like, but I try my hardest."

Think about it this way. Let's say I wanted to join your family. Could I become a member of your family by acting like you? What if I spent an hour a week at your house . . . say on Sunday morning? What if I dressed like the people in your family? Hung out with you? What if I just went around telling people I was part of your family?

None of those things would make me a member of your family. You can't think or act or work your way into a family. It's like saying, "Are you a Smith?"

"Oh, I try to live a good Smith-like life."
"Well, I hope so."
"I go to Smith's house."
"I like to think of myself as a Smith."
"I've been in Smith's swimming pool."
"I'm not as good of a Smith as I'd like, but I try my hardest."

It's stupid to talk like that. Being part of a family means being related to someone *despite, not because of* how you act.

It's the same with being part of God's family. Once you place your faith in Christ, the Bible says you have become part of God's family—you are born again (John 3:3) and adopted by God (Romans 8:15-17). Because of your good deeds? Nope. Because of the way you act or dress or how many prayer meetings or church services you attend? Nope. There is only one way into God's family: faith in Jesus Christ as your Savior.

And now, if you've placed your faith in Christ, you are ready to start living like a member of his family. That's one specific way you can live to honor the Spirit.

"He died for everyone so that those who receive his new life will no longer live to please themselves. Instead, they will live to please Christ, who died and was raised for them" (2 Corinthians 5:15).

Imagine that you gave someone a Christmas present and after she unwrapped it, she pulled out her purse and asked, "How much do I owe you?" You'd be insulted because you offered her a gift and you wouldn't expect her to pay you back!

It's the same with God. He gives us the gift of new life and welcomes us into his family through our faith. It's not our job to try and repay him. That would be insulting! Instead, our job is to grow closer to him, love and enjoy him, live a life of thanksgiving and bring him honor by our choices and lifestyle.

"Let your roots grow down into him and draw up nourishment from him, so you will grow in faith, strong and vigorous in the truth you were taught. Let your lives overflow with thanksgiving for all he has done" (Colossians 2:7).

When God sends his Spirit down to give new spiritual life, he also gives believers a new *lifestyle*. Being a believer is a process of growing in grace. We're saved by grace (Ephesians 2:8, 9), we live in grace (Romans 5:2) and we grow in grace (2 Peter 3:18). Each day we seek God and draw closer to him.

spiritual incense fifteen
we honor the Spirit when we seek his will and pursue our relationship with God

Christianity isn't a tradition. It isn't a religion. It isn't about going to church and trying your hardest to follow the rules. It isn't even about being good. It isn't about how you dress, who your parents are or how you act. Christianity is a relationship with Christ and a membership in God's family. Christianity is all about knowing, serving and honoring the God who loves you.

"God saved you by his special favor when you believed. And you can't take credit for this; it is a gift from God. Salvation is not a reward for the good things we have done, so none of us can boast about it" (Ephesians 2:8, 9).

Have you been trying to be good enough to be acceptable to God? Have you been trying to earn God's favor? Or pay him back by jumping through a bunch of spiritual hoops? When you become part of God's family, it's forever. And it doesn't depend on you, but on God.

The first step in honoring the Spirit is focusing on his grace and deepening your relationship with him. Being a child of God is a relationship that can't be severed, not a set of requirements that must be kept.

It's not at all what it first appears to be.

Because some things are not what they seem.

no artificial ingredients

What does it mean to let God lead me? What does prayer have to do with honoring the Spirit? What if I'm afraid to go where God leads me?

Clutching my Bible, I walked up the steps and raised my fist to knock on the door. Through the diamond-shaped window, I could see Chris and Tracy on the couch talking. Was this really the right thing to do? I held my hand in the air hoping I'd chicken out. But I couldn't shake the feeling that regardless of the consequences, we were doing the right thing.

"Well this is it. They'll probably never speak to me again after tonight," I said to my girlfriend Liesl, who was standing next to me.

"Are you sure you want to do this?" she asked.

"Yeah." I said, trying to convince myself.

I let my hand fall against the wood and watched as Chris gave Tracy an odd look, glanced at his watch and walked toward the door.

He swung open the door, flashed a surprised smile and cocked his head to the side. "Hey, Steve . . . What's the matter? Did you guys forget something?"

"Yeah," I replied, swallowing hard. "Could we come in?"

none of my business

I'd gone to school with Chris and Tracy but lost touch with them after we graduated. We used to hang out together because we were all into rock climbing and extreme sports. I can still see Tracy's splash of wild red hair bobbing halfway up the cliff and hear her infectious laughter echo around the campsite. And I can see Chris crashing along the rocky trail on his mountain bike at speeds that made your head spin. I didn't really notice it at the time, but now I remember they always brought just one tent along for the two of them.

So after graduation, we decided to get together over Thanksgiving.

"Let's go out for supper!" Tracy squealed into the phone. "Then afterwards, you guys can come over and see our apartment! You'll love it!"

Our apartment? She hadn't said *my* apartment. *Our* apartment?

"Okay, great. Um, we'll meet you at 6:00 P.M."

I remember hanging up the phone thinking, *They're probably living in separate rooms, just sharing the rent or something.* But I knew what the odds of that were, even though they both confessed to be Christians. I didn't know what to do. I mean, I knew what God thought of that kind of lifestyle, but was I the one to tell them? I wouldn't want to judge them or jump to conclusions. So, what if they were living together? It wasn't any of my business, was it?

I had this vague, almost nauseating, feeling in my stomach that God wanted me to talk to them about their lifestyle. It made me kind of sick because I didn't want to lose their friendship and I didn't want them to think I was some kind of religious lunatic. I mean, what else would they think if Liesl and I came barging into their lives and told them they were "living in sin"? What was I gonna do?

"you guys are gonna love our bedroom!"

Two hours later, Liesl and I were laughing with Chris and Tracy at a burger and shake place and I almost forgot about the whole apartment thing. We relived the old times, the camping trips we'd been on and rock climbing places we dreamed of visiting.

"Okay, you guys. Follow us home. We can have dessert and play board games!" Chris said, pushing back from the table.

Oh, boy. Here we go.

A few minutes later Tracy ushered us in and immediately began showing us around the place . . . the little kitchenette with the breakfast nook . . . Chris's weights and mountain bike in the garage . . . the cute little bathroom at the end of the hall.

"Oh! You guys are gonna love our bedroom!" Tracy gushed, "We have this waterbed that my parents helped us buy and it's awesome! C'mon, I'll show you!" She pushed open the bedroom door and plopped onto the waterbed, letting the waves sway her back and forth.

"Whaddya think? Pretty nice, huh?" Chris winked at me.

"Uh, yeah. It's great."

What was I supposed to say? Liesl looked at me expectantly, but I just slinked back to the living room. I wanted to say something, but I just didn't have the right words.

Then we talked about their new jobs and how Chris was sure he was gonna get into the Police Academy and was racing mountain bikes again. Tracy was working as a banquet planner and loved it. They were planning to get married in the spring. And on and on until we'd finished off dessert and listened to some music and played Taboo® and the conversation lulled and someone glanced at the clock . . .

"I guess we oughtta be going," I mumbled.

Chris stuck out his hand. "Well, thanks for coming over, you guys. It was great to see you again. Nice to meet you Liesl." We hugged and promised we'd write and then walked outside.

C'mon Steve, say something!

The next thing I knew the door was closed and I was starting the car. I knew I'd blown it. I knew God had wanted me to talk with them about their relationship with each other, and even more importantly, their relationship with him. But I hadn't. I'd let God down, and now I was too much of a coward to even go back there and make things right.

"what should we do?"

As I drove Liesl home, neither of us spoke. Outside, rain slashed against the windshield and bleary streetlights flashed past the car.

Finally, about 15 minutes into the drive. I blurted out, "Liesl how do you feel?"

She bounced the question right back into my court. "How do *you* feel?"

"I don't know. I kinda think God wanted us to talk to them."

"Me too. So, what are we gonna do?"

Good question. I had no idea what to do. Maybe I could call them sometime, or write them a letter or—

"Let's pray," she said.

"Huh?"

"Pray, you know. See what God wants us to do."

I hadn't thought of that. Even from the first time I heard about the apartment, I hadn't thought to pray about it. Maybe I was afraid God would use me to actually help answer my prayer.

I eased over to the shoulder of the highway and flipped on the four-way flashers. I couldn't believe we were doing this.

But there we sat, holding hands, talking to God with the cold November rain pounding the car. And it was weird. He didn't speak to us in some audible voice crackling over the radio, but something happened inside of us. When we asked him to send someone to talk with Chris and Tracy we knew in our hearts he had. Then we asked him what we should do.

Finally, we said "Amen."

Nothing much was different. Cars were still zooming by, freezing rain was still falling. But something inside of me was different.

"Let's go back," I said.

"Really?"

"Yeah. It won't be easy, but it'll be right."

So I turned the car around. Not because it made sense, not even because I wanted to. But because we couldn't shake the idea that God wanted us to go back. And, 45 minutes after we'd said "good night" we were there again, sitting in the living room, talking. For two hours we talked. We told them that God's plan was for sex to be reserved for marriage. They stared at us quietly.

And, since I knew that living together wasn't the real problem but only a symptom, we talked about what it means to have a relationship with God, not just to go to church and say you're a Christian. Sometimes I said the right things and sometimes the wrong ones.

At first, they just sat there sort of shocked. And then Chris was getting angry and I thought he was gonna throw us out. And then Tracy was crying and talking about how she felt far from God. And all this emotion—both good and bad—flooded the room. Real talk. Real feelings. And it only came out after we obeyed God and turned around.

the end of a friendship?

I'd like to tell you that everything ended on a happy note, that something dramatic happened, that they decided to move into different apartments and asked God to forgive them. But nothing like that happened. We kind of awkwardly said "good night" again, we stepped outside and Chris closed the door.

When we left that night, I thought our friendship with Chris and Tracy was over. I still cared about them just as much as I always had. But we went our separate ways and wrote occasionally. Then a few months later I got the letter in the mail.

Tracy wrote: *"Steve, after you guys left that night, Chris and I talked for a long time. We asked some of our friends and some of the pastors who live nearby and they all told us there was nothing wrong with what we are doing—sleeping together, you know. But we want to do what God wants, so we decided not to have sex again until after we're married in May. It'll be tough, but we think it's right. And, by the way, I've started reading the book of John in the Bible. I want to know more about God's plan and the Christian life."*

After I picked up my jaw, I sat down and reread the words.

Whoa.

That's when I realized how much of an impact that night had made on their lives. And how close I was to driving off and ignoring the Holy Spirit's prompting to talk to them.

what's the point?

"Don't act thoughtlessly, but try to understand what the Lord wants you to do. . . . let the Holy Spirit fill and control you" (Ephesians 5:17, 18).

When God talks to us, he prefers not to yell. He whispers. He nudges. We need to be tuned in to find out where he wants us to go. And we need to respond.

A man named Philip was one of the leaders in the early church. He witnessed to an Ethiopian treasurer, who became the first Christian convert from the continent of Africa. Philip was tuned in to God. He listened and acted and God put him in the right place at the right time. And then Philip took action. Read his story in Acts 8:26-40.

Today, God speaks to us first and foremost through the Bible. Whatever the Bible says is clearly God's will. But his Spirit also communicates directly with our hearts, giving us direction and guidance day by day: *"He renews my strength. He guides me along right paths, bringing honor to his name"* (Psalm 23:3).

One of the keys to honoring the Spirit with our lives is listening and responding to God when he speaks to us—even if it doesn't seem to make sense. God guides us in Bible study, genuine worship and heartfelt prayer.

what does it mean to pray?

Prayer has nothing to do with secret formulas or chanting like a monk or saying words like "Thee" or "Thou" or "In the Name of Jesus." It isn't even the words that are important—it's what's in your heart that counts. Real prayer honors God, *"I will honor you as long as I live, lifting up my hands to you in prayer" (Psalm 63:4).*

When we pray we talk to God, but there's more to it than that. Prayer is more of a lifestyle than an activity. That's why God encourages us to "pray continually" (1 Thessalonians 5:17, NIV) and live lives of "constant prayer" (Luke 18:1). Because prayer is being real before God.

That means no pretending. No acting like you're good enough, respectable enough or wise enough on your own that you don't need God. No games, no role-playing, no masks, no excuses. Be genuine. Be vulnerable, honest, sincere and authentic.

"But you desire honesty from the heart, so you can teach me to be wise in my inmost being" (Psalm 51:6).

I used to go bow hunting. When you hunt deer with a bow and arrow, you need to camouflage yourself so the deer don't notice you. And one of the ways you do that is with special oils that mask your scent. You can actually fool the deer into thinking you're something you're not—another deer.

That's what some people do with God. They try to fool him. But it won't work. He can always tell the difference between the real fragrance of faith and the fake scents of hypocrisy.

Jesus saved his harshest words for the people who pretended to be religious, but had no inner peace with God: "*These people honor me with their lips, but their hearts are far away. Their worship is a farce"* (Mark 7:7). Those people acted like they were close to God, but their hearts were nowhere near him. They were living artificial lives.

> *"The LORD's searchlight penetrates the human spirit, exposing every hidden motive" (Proverbs 20:27).*

The closer you get to someone, the better you can tell what he really smells like. The closer you get to God, the better you'll be able to tell what he really smells like. And the more you'll begin to carry the scent of God into your life.

you can live an authentic life by being:

- Honest—by keeping your promises.
- Sincere—by meaning what you say.
- Respectful—by showing that you care.
- Vulnerable—by admitting when you're wrong.

When you pray, you're not on stage, putting on a show or standing in the spotlight. No acting allowed. You're not playing a part. You're opening yourself up to God and asking for his guidance and direction.

> *"But when you pray, go away by yourself, shut the door behind you, and pray to your Father secretly. Then your Father, who knows all secrets, will reward you" (Matthew 6:6).*

When it seems like God has abandoned you, tell him so! When you flunk a test, say something stupid, run out of money or don't know where to turn, ask God what to do.

When you're filled with sadness, let it overflow to him. When you're angry or afraid or hurting or confused, let him know. When you're stressed out or in trouble, talk to God. That's real prayer. But don't pretend. If there's anyone in all creation who can sniff out the truth, it's God.

Praise God for who he is. Thank God for all he's done. And on those days when God's love just overwhelms you and you can't seem to hold it in, let loose! Explode into passionate praise and thanksgiving without fear of embarrassment!

That's what being real is all about.

"Yes, what joy for those whose record the LORD cleared of sin, whose lives are lived in complete honesty!" (Psalm 32:2).

Live before God with complete honesty and he will use you in mighty ways to impact the world. Stop pretending and start listening and responding. Submit to God's word and his guidance. Just like Philip did.

Rely on God's strength and resources to live a godly life. It's easy to get in God's way. Instead, trust him and let the Holy Spirit fill you and direct your life. God isn't looking for your *ability*, but your *availability*. God is more interested in your reliance and submission than your resources and strength.

Living real, honest, open lives is tough. But that's what God asks us to do. Honesty from the heart shows people that God has made a real difference in your life. Inside and out.

Real prayer and heartfelt worship, with no artificial ingredients, smells sweet to God. Stop pretending with God and start living the real life.

spiritual incense sixteen
▬ we honor the Spirit when we prayerfully let God guide us in the choices we make every day

Where are Chris and Tracy today? I'm not sure. But one thing I do know, whenever I think of them, I think of what Jesus said about asking, seeking and knocking. When we ask, he answers. When we seek, he lets us find. And when we knock, he opens up doors. Even when we're most afraid the door will slam in our face, he holds it open and, if we're willing to step through, he does amazing things.

And when we mess up or start heading in the wrong direction, turning to him is the only way to get the strength to turn around. Prayer is more than just talking to God. It also has to do with listening to him and being available. Because sometimes *we* are the doors God uses to help our friends find his love.

I'm glad I knocked on that door after all.

death by vending machine

How can I be successful and still serve God? What does it mean to store up treasures in Heaven? How can I use my life to honor God?

Recently, when I was getting a soda from a vending machine, I noticed a small sign on the upper right-hand corner of the machine: "Never rock or tilt! Machine can fall over and cause serious injury or death."

I started thinking, *Whoa! . . . Death by vending machine. What an embarrassing way to die . . .*

It reminded me of my high school biology teacher. When we were studying infectious diseases, he'd always get this weird look in his eyes and say, "Ya'll gonna die, baby!" Then he'd start scanning the room looking at different students, "Five of you are gonna die from cancer . . . three of you are gonna die from AIDS . . . four of you are gonna die in car accidents . . . one of you is gonna kill yourself . . . but ya'll gonna die, baby!" (He never mentioned death by vending machine.)

And then he'd laugh with this evil mad scientist laugh and head off to dissect something. I think he'd been in the lab too long.

And yet, as funny as my biology teacher seemed to think it was, death is no laughing matter.

Death is the world's greatest tragedy. And none of us knows when our life is going to end. It might be tomorrow. It might be today. But we are all gonna die. My biology teacher had that much right.

"LORD, remind me how brief my time on earth will be. Remind me that my days are numbered, and that my life is fleeing away" (Psalm 39:4).

One of the keys to smelling like God is realizing how fragile and short life is. Listen to how Solomon puts it, *"Yes, remember your Creator now while you are young, before the silver cord of life snaps and the golden bowl is broken" (Ecclesiastes 12:6).*

Life is short. It passes away before you even notice. So how are you gonna spend your time? What would make for a successful life?

The only treasures that will last are things we've done for God's honor, not our own. People who pursue only earthly treasures are no better off than roadkill, *"They may name their estates after themselves, but they leave their wealth to others. They will not last long despite their riches—they will die like the animals" (Psalm 49:11, 12).*

To die like the animals. How sad it would be to die only to find out that you had wasted your life. That it slipped by without you even realizing it, and you never took advantage of the many chances you had to honor the God who loves you.

As one poet put it, "Some men die in battle, some men die in flames. But most men perish inch by inch while playing little games."

Don't spend your life playing little games. Spend it smelling like God.

"Live wisely among those who are not Christians, and make the most of every opportunity" (Colossians 4:5).

my definite chief aim

Before *Crouching Tiger, Hidden Dragon*, Bruce Lee was one of the greatest martial arts superstars of all time. He was in dozens of Chinese movies and five major American releases. Bruce Lee was legendary around the world for his incredibly quick reflexes and amazing kung fu moves.

Yet, one of the most eye-opening things Bruce Lee did isn't even in one of his movies. It's a note that he wrote to himself when he was 29 years old. You can see it hanging in a framed case on the second floor of Planet Hollywood in downtown Nashville, Tennessee.

> *My Definite Chief Aim*
>
> *I, Bruce Lee, will be the first highest paid Oriental superstar in the United States. In return I will give the most exciting performances and render the best of quality in the capacity of an actor. Starting in 1970 I will achieve world fame and from then onward till the end of 1980 I will have in my possession $10,000,000. I will live the way I please and achieve inner harmony and happiness.*
>
> *Bruce Lee*
> *January, 1969*

Bruce Lee was born in 1940 and never lived to see the end of this goal. He died in his sleep in 1973. He was 33 years old.

what will i do with all this dough?

There's nothing wrong with committing yourself to excellence, striving to reach lofty goals or working your hardest—those are things God wants each of us to do. And maybe God has called you to be an actor, a superstar or a martial arts sensation—great! But whatever God has in mind for you to do, it should be done for *God's* honor.

Bruce Lee committed himself to something else. Something that doesn't last—his own fortune and glory. Look again at the "definite chief aim" of his life. He wanted to become the "highest paid Oriental superstar," "achieve world fame," accumulate "$10,000,000," and live the way he pleased.

Someone long ago had similar goals to Bruce Lee. Jesus told a story about him. He was a rich guy who had more money than he knew what to do with. He decided he'd just keep adding bigger and bigger barns to hold all his dough and store all his toys. He'd made it to the top of the ladder of success without even realizing it was leaning against the wrong building. Then one day he retired early to live it up, take it easy and party.

But God had a different plan. That very night God took the rich guy's life. Unexpectedly. In his sleep. Because God didn't want anyone around who was committed to living only for himself. Read the story for yourself in Luke 12:15-20.

Jesus warned, *"Beware! Don't be greedy for what you don't have. Real life is not measured by how much we own. . . . Yes, a person is a fool to store up earthly wealth but not have a rich relationship with God" (Luke 12:15, 21).*

Those are powerful words. Another time Jesus put it like this: *"Don't store up treasures here on earth, where they can be eaten by moths and get rusty, and where thieves break in and steal. Store your treasures in heaven, where they will never become moth-eaten or rusty and where they will be safe from thieves. Wherever your treasure is, there your heart and thoughts will also be" (Matthew 6:19-21).*

Treasures on earth or treasures in Heaven? Where are you storing your treasures? In the sand castle down on the shore, or in the mansion up on the hill? Where are your thoughts? Where is your heart?

When Jesus talked about treasures in Heaven, he meant that we will be rewarded for the selfless deeds we did, the Spirit-led actions we took and the love-motivated words we spoke here on earth.

You can't take stuff with you into the afterlife. So stop trying to store it up on earth! Instead, spend your time and energy deepening and enriching your relationship with God. And store up rewards in Heaven by making God-honoring choices here on earth.

the real secret of success

Most people spend their life working in a job they don't like, for a boss they don't respect, with people they don't get along with, to make the money to buy stuff they don't even need. And if they endure this lifestyle long enough, we call them a success!

Jesus called John the Baptist the greatest man to ever live. And what was his life philosophy? *"He [Jesus] must become greater and greater, and I must become less and less" (John 3:30).* He wanted to become less and less visible as Jesus took over more and more of his life. And Jesus called him the greatest man who ever lived.

the world says . . .	God Says . . .
"You need to find yourself."	"You're lost . . . I need to find you."
"Follow your heart!"	"Your heart is deceitful . . . follow me."
"Love yourself!"	"Hate your old self . . . love me instead."
"Do what you want!"	"Deny yourself . . . do what I want."
"Be all you can be!"	"Let me fill you . . . and be more than you can be."
"Whoever dies with the most toys, wins!"	"Get your priorities straight. . . Whoever dies without me, loses."

When God measures success, he doesn't ask, "How much have you earned?" He asks, "How faithful have you been?" Because you can never be a success unless Christ is at the center of your life. You will never be rich by clinging to the things of this world.

"And how do you benefit if you gain the whole world but lose your own soul in the process? Is anything worth more than your soul?" (Matthew 16:26).

The way to achieve true inner harmony and happiness isn't by earning a mountain of cash, or impressing hordes of fans or even seeing your name in lights. True harmony, happiness and peace come from knowing your sins are forgiven and that you are accepted by God—despite the mistakes and the wrongs you've done in the past.

Then you can move on to following, serving and honoring the God who loves you by letting go of the things of this life and clinging to the hope of the life to come; by being faithful to him, putting him first and trusting him for eternal results.

In the book of Ecclesiastes, Solomon explores the mysteries and meaning of life. He concludes that without God at the heart of the matter, life is meaningless. Four thoughts echo throughout the book:

- Obey God, for this is the duty of every person (Ecclesiastes 12:13).
- Enjoy life, even though it is brief and filled with uncertainty (Ecclesiastes 3:12, 13).
- Work hard, though it sometimes seems tiring and useless (Ecclesiastes 5:12, 16-20).
- Be content, because wealth will never bring happiness (Ecclesiastes 5:8-15; 6:9).

In God's eyes, a successful life is one of obedience, enjoyment, integrity and contentment. Build your life on those four pillars and, even though no one else may notice, God will call you a success.

spiritual incense seventeen
we honor the Spirit when we make the most of each day and value heavenly things above earthly ones

There are lots of philosophies out there about how to get rich quick or lead a successful life. But true success only comes from knowing God and following his will. The secret to being successful in God's eyes is by studying Scripture, and applying it in your life.

Bruce Lee made a vow to live for himself. Maybe it's time you made a resolution as well. Not like Bruce Lee's, seeking fortune and glory. Not even something like deciding to eat fewer candy bars, or floss every day or sweep under your bed before the dust bunnies rise up in revolt. Instead, commit yourself to living each day for God.

It won't be easy. You'll be tempted to fix your eyes on all the stuff around you. But through prayer, worship, Bible study and hanging with Christian friends you can focus on the stuff that really matters. The stuff that lasts. Set your mind on things above, not on earthly things. Trust in God and honor him with your life. That's what makes him happy.

"The LORD's delight is in those who honor him, those who put their hope in his unfailing love" (Psalm 147:11).

Take some time today to write your own "Definite Chief Aim" in the space below. Think about what kind of a life would really honor God.

Do it today. Before the silver cord of your life snaps. Store up treasures in Heaven. Make yourself a vow today that will matter. Forever.

My Definite Chief Aim,

scarred for life

Where is God when bad things happen? How can I honor God when life sucks? How come there's so much pain and sadness in the world? How does that honor God?

Every time I wore a T-shirt someone would stare. Every time I showered in gym class or changed clothes after track practice I could feel their eyes tracing the ragged scars around my neck, across my chest, and down my left arm. And when I looked up, everyone turned away and pretended like they hadn't been staring at me.

But they were.

Oh, sure, sometimes they'd ask the question, "Hey, how did you get all those scars?"

But mostly they just stared.

And I couldn't help asking a few questions myself: *Why did God let this happen to me? Why didn't he just end my life all those years ago? What possible reason could God have for letting a helpless baby get fried by hot grease?*

Then one day when I was 19 years old, I met Brad.

"Hey, Steve, how'd you get those scars?"

I sighed and turned around. The same old question. I was tired of answering it and was just about ready to give some smart-aleck response when I saw who was standing there.

It was a kid who looked about nine years old. He'd combed his long hair to the side, across his head. He wore a long-sleeve shirt and sweatpants even though it was 90 degrees outside. I could tell he was hiding something.

So I told him the truth. "Well, when I was eleven months old my mom was cooking french fries in a deep fat fryer, I pulled the cord and the whole thing slid off the counter. A gallon of boiling-hot grease poured onto my head." I pulled up my sleeve to show him the extent of the scarring on my left arm. I showed him the scars on my neck and across my chest. "I almost died that day," I added.

"You aren't gonna believe this!" Brad exclaimed. "When I was eight months old, my sister was cooking french fries and I pulled the cord and the hot grease poured on me!"

He tipped his head to the side revealing a large scar covering half of his scalp. "And I have one on my arm and here on my leg." He pointed to his shin.

No way! It was just like me! Same cord-pulling-grease-splattering-scenario!

We talked for awhile. I told him I knew how it felt to be stared at, but that it doesn't really change who you are underneath. "You don't need to be embarrassed or ashamed, the scars are just a part of who you are," I said. And when he walked away, he was smiling.

I saw him later that week wearing shorts.

Huh.

No one else he'd ever met could quite understand how it felt to go through life with scars like that. But I could help, because I had the same scars.

For as long as I could remember I'd been asking God, "Why? Why did you let this happen?!" And that day I finally heard an answer: *Sometimes God uses the wounds in one life to heal the pain in another.*

We all have scars. Some are on the surface. Some are in our hearts, where no one but God can see. Deep, deep scars. Scars from those words you accidentally overheard . . . from the apology that was never given . . . from the tears you bottled up and never cried . . . from the shattered dreams or broken heart you carry. But instead of blindly asking, "Why?" open your eyes and ask, "Who else?" Odds are, someday you'll meet someone with the same scars. Will you be ready to help that person? Will you let God bring something good out of the scars in your life?

God used the years of questioning, struggling and wondering to prepare me for that moment when I would meet that little nine-year-old boy. Be ready. He'll be able to use your scars for something good, too.

why me, God? ━━━━━━━━━━━ what's the point?

Why does God let bad things happen? Well, sometimes to heal the wounds in other lives, sometimes to draw us closer to himself, sometimes to test us, strengthen our faith or humble us. And sometimes to teach us to rely more on him and less on ourselves. Suffering can actually be a wake-up call to renew our commitment to honoring God:

> *"I used to wander off until you disciplined me; but now I closely follow your word. . . . The suffering you sent was good for me, for it taught me to pay attention to your principles" (Psalm 119:67, 71).*

Yet, sometimes God doesn't reveal why he allows us to suffer. When Job lost everything, he begged God for an answer concerning why he was suffering, but God didn't give him one. God just told Job to be quiet, quit questioning his wisdom and trust in him. Finally, Job did just that (Job 40:4, 5), and God blessed him for it (42:12).

God knows bad things are gonna happen. Pain and suffering come with living in a sin-stained world. He doesn't want us to pretend that we have all the answers or that we don't sometimes question why things happen the way they do. Even Jesus asked "Why?" He cried out from the cross, *"My God, my God, why have you forsaken me?" (Mark 15:34).*

But God does ask us to submit to him and let him call the shots. And he wants us to get busy using our own stories, life experiences and personality to shine in the darkness of this fallen and hurting world. No matter what happens.

We honor God when we stick with him, trust that he knows best and remain faithful even when life doesn't make sense.

> *"We serve God whether people honor us or despise us, whether they slander us or praise us" (2 Corinthians 6:8).*

How should we respond when bad things happen? What kind of reaction pleases God? Even though God doesn't always explain why bad things happen, the Bible does give us guidance on how to respond when hard times come.

1. stop hating others for the evil things they do

The abuse started when Naomi was four years old. When she was 12, she was raped. And it didn't stop. It happened again and again. Finally, when she was 17 years old, she called the police to turn in her own stepfather.

He was eventually convicted on 25 counts of sexual abuse. Naomi, now a Christian, finds it hard to forgive him for what he did. But she has learned to accept what happened and move on. "I'll never forget it or be happy," she says. "I can't change the past. I don't hate him any more. I have an acceptance."

If Naomi can stop hating the man who raped her more than two dozen times, you certainly can let go of any hatred in your heart, too. *"Get rid of all bitterness, rage, anger, harsh words, and slander, as well as all types of malicious behavior. Instead, be kind to each other, tenderhearted, forgiving one another, just as God through Christ has forgiven you" (Ephesians 4:31, 32).*

2. trust that God can bring about something good, even when bad things happen

Joseph had every right to hold a grudge.

His brothers hated him and made fun of him. One day they decided to kill him, but at the last moment opted to sell him as a slave instead. Joseph became a household servant in a foreign land and was soon imprisoned for a crime he didn't commit.

His brothers thought they'd never see him again.

But after many years, God brought them back together. And this time, the tables were turned. Now, Joseph (who'd become a high-ranking government official) held *their* lives in *his* hands. He had the chance to get even, but didn't. Instead of seeking revenge he invited the whole family to move in with him.

His brothers were terrified. They knew Joseph might one day pay them back for the way they'd treated him. So they begged him not to retaliate. *"But Joseph told them, 'Don't be afraid of me. Am I God, to judge and punish you? As far as I am concerned, God turned into good what you meant for evil.' . . . And he spoke very kindly to them, reassuring them"* (Genesis 50:19-21).

Joseph wasn't out for revenge. He saw a bigger plan at work. He realized God was in control behind the scenes. He certainly had the chance to cling to unforgiveness and revenge, but chose instead to forgive and trust in God. Because of his faith, Joseph was able to let go of bitterness and open his arms to those who'd hurt him.

Forgiving others isn't easy, but it is possible. When you've been wronged, remind yourself how willing God was to forgive you, then lean on his promises and his love rather than on your own feelings. God can remove even the most bitter grudge, if you let him.

Trust that God is in control, even when terrible things happen.

> *"And we know that God causes everything to work together for the good of those who love God and are called according to his purpose for them" (Romans 8:28).*

3. leave the matter in God's hands

Samson was always trying to get even. *"'Because you did this,' Samson vowed, 'I will take my revenge on you, and I won't stop until I'm satisfied!'" (Judges 15:7).* Eventually, his desire for revenge consumed and destroyed him.

Don't try to get even. Let God take care of vengeance. You take care of forgiveness. *"Dear friends, never avenge yourselves. Leave that to God" (Romans 12:19).*

4. let go of your bitterness

Love keeps no record of wrongs (1 Corinthians 13:5) so, when the people of Lystra stoned Paul and left him for dead, the first thing he did when he gained consciousness was return to visit the people who'd just tried to kill him! A few days later he went back to strengthen the believers in Lystra, encourage them in their faith and remind them that life isn't easy. No kidding!

Paul wasn't bitter, either toward those who tried to kill him or toward God. You too can let go of bitterness when life stinks. When you're hurt, treated unfairly or suffer unjustly, you're given the choice—lock up the anger and bitterness, or let God have it and move on.

what Jesus left behind

Jesus came to bring peace. But it's not the world's kind of peace. Jesus brings inner peace that doesn't depend on circumstances, but on relationship. True peace comes from having your sins forgiven and knowing that whatever comes your way, God will never abandon you.

As Paul wrote in Romans 5:1, *"Therefore, since we have been made right in God's sight by faith, we have peace with God because of what Jesus Christ our Lord has done for us."* And that kind of peace will spread the right kind of fragrance to everyone you meet.

Jesus said,

> *"I am leaving you with a gift—peace of mind and heart. And the peace I give isn't like the peace the world gives. So don't be troubled or afraid. Remember what I told you: I am going away, but I will come back to you again" (John 14:27, 28).*

Yeah, troubles will come. Bad things will happen. But when they do, you have the opportunity to lean on Jesus, learn from him and rely more fully on God.

Peace isn't the absence of trouble or conflict. Jesus never promised us that life would be easy. Instead, he made it clear that believers will face lots of tough times (Matthew 24:9, 10). But he won't leave us alone. His peace is present in our hearts.

And most amazing of all, he is with us always—day by day—forever. As Jesus told his followers, *"And be sure of this: I am with you always, even to the end of the age" (Matthew 28:19, 20).*

spiritual incense eighteen
we honor the Spirit when we continue to trust in God even when life doesn't make sense

God will be with you. Through the tough times. Through the good times. Through the bad times. You may never see the full purpose of suffering in this life, but you can honor the Holy Spirit by continuing to trust in him even when life—with all of its suffering—doesn't make sense.

I waited 18 years for my scars (and my God) to make sense. My questions were finally answered one day when I glimpsed a nine-year-old boy running toward the beach wearing only his swimming suit, his hair whipping freely in the breeze.

when eddie flipped the switch

What's the big deal about sex? Why can't God just understand that it's fun and everybody's doing it these days?

The dampness of the August night sent a chill through the air. In the distance, frogs sang to the moonlight. I reached for Kathy's hand and, as our fingers met and intertwined, she leaned against my shoulder and held me. The night no longer seemed so cold.

I'd only known Kathy for six days, but from the moment we first met, I knew there'd be something special between us. All week I'd tried to find opportunities to be alone with her. Now, finally, on the last night of camp we were able to get together outside the Lodge.

a different set of rules

We'd been talking for over an hour, yet it seemed like not even a moment had slipped by.

"Hey, Kathy," I whispered.

"Yeah?"

"What happens tomorrow? Do we have to say good-bye?"

"We never have to say good-bye," she said, easing closer. "And besides, it's already *tomorrow*."

"You mean it's after midnight?"

"Yeah. Why?"

I hesitated for a moment. "Well, I didn't realize it was so late. We should get back to our cabins."

"The kids can wait. I just want to sit here with you. . . . And, besides, everyone else is at the Lodge playing cards."

Oh, man. The way she peered at me with those blue eyes, the way she tucked her golden hair back from her face, her infectious laughter . . . It was all I could do to tell her we needed to go back to our cabins.

"But . . . curfew is midnight."

"Actually mine is 11:30," she said slyly. "Remember I'm only an *assistant* counselor."

"Oh, yeah. Then I guess we should—"

She turned and stared at me in the moonlight. "I should have known. You always follow the rules, don't you?" She leaned forward slowly until she was only a few inches from my face, her fingers tightening their grip on my hand. My hands started to sweat and my heart began racing. More than anything else I wanted to kiss her. And she knew it.

"Goodnight, Steve," she mouthed, and then glided to her feet. "I wouldn't want to get you in trouble." Before she disappeared down the trail she turned to flash me her smile.

I gulped. If anyone could get me into trouble, it was Kathy. When I was with her it as like I was under her control. And she played by a different set of rules, I'd learned that much already. Maybe that's why I was so attracted to her, because I knew she didn't have the same limits I had.

I sighed and walked toward my cabin with different voices speaking in my head: *You made the right decision, it was time to say goodnight. Now you can look forward to seeing her again next time . . . There might not be a next time. You might have lost Kathy tonight! Maybe you shouldn't worry so much about following the rules. No one else does.*

"aren't you cold?"

After camp, we kept in touch. When she wrote to invite me to the staff reunion the weekend after Christmas, I decided not to reply, but to surprise her when I got there.

When I arrived at the Lodge, everything looked so different. Without a hundred kids running around, without leaves or tents or volleyball courts, the camp looked desolate. Snow covered everything. And more snow was gently falling from heavy gray clouds. I headed downstairs and threw my sleeping bag on an empty bunk.

"Yo, Steve!" a voice thundered at me from across the room.

"Hey, Eddie," I called back.

A huge college wrestler wrapped me in his arms and squeezed. You never forgot one of Eddie's hugs. Eddie had been a counselor in my unit the summer before. He'd been attending camp forever.

"Who's all here so far?" I asked.

"You looking for someone in particular?" he said smiling.

"Well, actually . . . I'm looking for Kathy."

"Are you guys . . .?" He let his voice trail off suggestively.

"No. Not really. I mean, we're not." I stuttered.

"Right. She's upstairs."

"Thanks, Eddie. I'll see you later." I smiled at him and headed upstairs to find Kathy.

From the top of the staircase I could see her entering the Lodge. She paused at the door to shake snow out of her hair. Then our eyes met.

"Steve!"

I went to her waiting arms and remembered again the night in August. Something deep within me stirred, something that was at the same time frightening and exciting.

"Merry Christmas, Kathy, it's good to see you again."

"Ditto." She winked at me, "Did you bring me anything?"

I pulled out the package I'd tucked under my coat. "Of course!"

And for the rest of the day we flew down Campfire Hill on the toboggan, clinging to each other and tumbling purposely into snow piles. We sipped hot apple cider lounging around the Lodge. We walked along the powdery trails as fresh flakes slowly covered our tracks. Most of all we talked. And laughed.

After supper everyone played games and Eddie showed a video he'd made during the summer. Then we sat around talking until someone popped in a video. Kathy nestled up next to me.

"Aren't you cold?" she asked.

"Cold? No. Are you?" I turned to face her, but she'd already gone to get a blanket.

The blanket she brought back was just the right size for two people.

We slipped to the back of the room and lay down on the floor with our backs up against the couch. I tucked the blanket over her legs and up to her chin.

After a little while, she leaned close to my ear. "I'm still cold, Steve," she whispered.

My heart was racing. *Stop, right now! Go sit up front with everyone else. Don't play this game, she plays by another set of rules . . . Gimme a break! What rules? You're not doing anything wrong. All she wants you to do is sit by her!*

I'd listened to that first voice in August, and where had it gotten me? So, I pulled the blanket up over my body and snuggled next to her. She wrapped herself around me.

no rules . . . no rules . . .

By now we were paying less and less attention to the movie. In fact, we were pretty oblivious to everything but each other.

"Still cold," Kathy muttered invitingly, twisting her neck to look into my eyes.

No Steve, you're gonna regret this. Be careful, say "no" while you still can!

"Here," I said, slipping her hand under my shirt. "Is that warmer?"

She held me tight, moving her arm slowly across my chest.

"Steve, you're surprising me," she purred. "You're not cold at all."

By now we'd slid down so we were laying together on the floor, under the blanket. Time slipped by. Minutes. Maybe hours.

"I can feel your heart beating. Thump. Thump. Thump," she whispered.

"Yeah."

"Thump, thump, thump."

There's no curfew tonight, Steve, no rules. No rules . . .

"Thump, thump, thump."

No rules . . . No rules . . .

I turned to kiss her as her hand glided down my stomach and found my belt buckle. I closed my eyes and just before our lips met, the credits ended. Eddie flipped on the lights. "Okay, everyone! Time for beddy-bye! Everyone off to bed, it's almost 3:00 in the morning!"

Kathy and I quickly and awkwardly untangled our bodies from under the blanket and stood up brushing ourselves off.

"I'm heading downstairs. You coming, Steve?" Eddie called.

"See you tomorrow, Eddie. I'll get the lights." I replied without looking away from Kathy.

Say goodnight Steve. Walk away!

"That's okay, I can wait," Eddie said.

Finally, I said to her, "Kathy . . ."

Ask her to meet you somewhere privately, to continue where you left off . . .

"Yes?" she answered, still breathing heavily.

"Um . . ."

Which voice? Which voice should I follow?

I gulped. "Goodnight, I'll see you tomorrow."

For a long time she looked at me curiously, the fire fading from her eyes. "It is tomorrow," she finally responded.

Then she shook her head, "All right. Good-bye, Steve."

I hadn't expected her to say good-bye. But the way she looked at me when she turned, the chill in her voice—I knew she meant it. She stomped upstairs to the women's loft.

"C'mon, Steve, it's time for bed," Eddie said as I watched Kathy go.

And a romance that had never really gotten started, ended. Our lips had never touched, yet I knew we'd been on the verge of going way too far. And even though part of me was sorry and wanted to call her back and offer to make it all up to her, I knew I shouldn't. I realized I'd almost made a huge mistake, a mistake I would have regretted for a long time. I also learned something shocking about myself that night. Something that woke me up and changed my dating habits forever. As I walked toward the stairs leading down to my bunk I realized I wouldn't have stopped if the lights had stayed off.

Someday I ought to thank Eddie for flipping that switch.

what's the point?

"Don't let anyone think less of you because you are young. Be an example to all believers in what you teach, in the way you live, in your love, your faith, and your purity" (1 Timothy 4:12).

Let's face it, it's tough to be an example of purity in today's world. Everywhere you look—school, TV, movies, magazines—people are acting like sex outside of marriage is the norm.

But not according to God. God invented sex. It's a natural, necessary and wonderful part of life. But God *only* intended sex to be part of a lifelong marriage relationship between one man and one woman (Matthew 19:5).

God knew what he was doing. And he knew the best way to give maximum pleasure and fulfillment in sex was to keep it preserved within the marriage relationship. When you step outside of God's will, you have to deal with the fear of getting caught, the shame of knowing you should have said "no," the regrets for what you did and the pressure to go a little further next time. But God's way is different. His plan is for purity, freedom and innocence.

> *"For God bought you with a high price. So you must honor God with your body" (1 Corinthians 6:20).*

God doesn't look lightly on sexual sin. It's so serious that, in Jesus' day, the penalty for sleeping around was death (John 8:4, 5).

Sex outside of marriage is wrong. Plain and simple. Even fantasizing about it is wrong (Matthew 5:28). Purity starts in your heart and your mind, so God wants you to think about what is pure and lovely, not what is suggestive and crude (Philippians 4:8).

Keep a clear conscience and don't push the limits. If you're getting so passionate with your girlfriend that you can't seem to stop, you've gone too far (see Song of Songs 8:4 and 1 John 3:21).

God desires purity. *"God wants you to be holy, so you should keep clear of all sexual sin" (1 Thessalonians 4:3).* Keeping clear of all sexual sin includes lust, pornography, masturbation, homosexuality and any sexual touch or intimacy outside of marriage.

Each day we face a choice: either to honor the Spirit, or indulge ourselves. It's part of our job as believers to find out what pleases God and then pursue it (Galatians 6:7, 8). Start doing that, today.

what if i've already done it?

Okay, so God desires purity. That much we know. But what if you've already done it? What if it's already too late for you?

What's done is done. You can't go back and undo it. Physically you can't start over again.

But in a real sense you can start over again, spiritually: *"If we confess our sins to him, he is faithful and just to forgive us and to cleanse us from every wrong" (1 John 1:9).*

You made a mistake. You blew it. So admit it. Go to God for forgiveness. And trust that he will forgive you. Then commit yourself to sexual purity and move on. God will cleanse you and give you a fresh start.

Don't let your conscience be controlled by the mistakes of the past. It's time for freedom. And a new commitment to God.

Take a minute right now and talk to God about the relational and sexual choices you've made. If you need to, ask him for the forgiveness, strength and purity to start over. And then trust in his promises to hear, forgive and strengthen you.

how far is too far?

It's easy to set yourself up for failure when you're dating (or courting) someone. It's a lot better to have some guidelines set up before you're alone and in the heat of temptation. Here are a few of the guidelines I started using to keep me from going too far:

1. only cuddle standing up

As soon as you lay down with someone and start cuddling under a blanket you'll start telling yourself it's okay to go further than you should. Don't do it. No horizontal hugging.

2. remember the "swimming suit principle"

One girl told me that dating a certain guy was like going out with an octopus. "He had his hands all over me!" she said. So how much touching is okay? The Bible puts it this way, *"among you there must not be even a hint of sexual immorality" (Ephesians 5:3, NIV).* If you're touching each other all over, there's more than a hint going on! If you want a good guideline, agree not to touch each other anywhere that a swimming suit would cover.

3. plan your dates

Sitting around watching TV isn't much of a date. Since you're not talking ('cause the TV is on) and you're not really doing anything, the only way to connect with each other is by getting physical. Instead, plan your dates. Study together. Go mountain biking. Make her supper. Always have something positive and active to do.

4. keep the lights on

You know how it is when you flick off the lights—temptation kicks into overdrive. Hormonal meltdown. So don't set yourself up for failure, keep the lights on.

5. stick to group dates

When you're alone with your date, it's easy to start doing things you'd never do in a group. Groups give you accountability. Sure, you'll need to be alone sometimes, but don't do it in an isolated setting. Be alone in public.

6. only date christians

You can see by my story what can happen when the person you're dating has different standards than you do. Let your faith bring you together and then pursue purity together. Dating someone for his or her looks is like buying a car based on the paint job. Only an idiot would do that. Look for inner beauty instead (1 Peter 3:4).

"How can a young person stay pure? By obeying your word and following its rules" (Psalm 119:9).

spiritual incense nineteen
we honor the Spirit when we pursue purity in our thoughts, words and actions

When you look at an ocean, all you can see is the surface. But underneath the waves there are lots of currents going in all different directions.

God sees beneath the surface to the underlying currents in your life. And Jesus wants purity all the way down—in your emotions, your thoughts and your desires. He wants purity of heart, mind and will. To God, being faithful in little things is a big thing.

So ask yourself, "Are my thoughts pure? Are my motives pure? Are my actions reflecting society's values, or God's? Do the things I do with my boyfriend really honor God?"

"Let us cleanse ourselves from everything that can defile our body or spirit. And let us work toward complete purity because we fear God" (2 Corinthians 7:1).

God wants us to filter out the kind of thoughts, words and deeds that would cause us to be impure. Purity is a choice. And it's never too late to start making choices (and setting limits) that honor God.

who'll ever know?

If God always forgives me, why should I even obey him? Why should I be good?

As I rounded a bend in the trail winding through the dense forest, I froze. Two young men about my age sat blocking the path. I'd hiked this trail lots of times before and I'd never seen anyone else in this part of the woods. My heart began to race as I saw what they were doing.

They were smoking marijuana.

Both of them looked up at me quickly as I stepped around the bend, but when they saw how old I was, they relaxed again. One of them said, "Hey, man, I don't know if you're into this or not, but do you want some?"

the choice

I stood there and looked around. *Did I want some?* We were in the middle of a forest that stretched for miles. These guys had chosen a nice remote spot for getting high. No one would see us. If I sat down to smoke with them, I knew I wouldn't get caught.

Did I want some?

No one would find out if I tried a little. I mean, who would ever know? I sure wouldn't tell. And I'd never see these two guys again.

Up until then I'd always steered clear of drugs and alcohol. Once, right after entering high school, my dad had pulled me aside and told me, "Now, a lot of your friends are gonna start drinking and I don't want you to embarrass yourself and our family by going out with them and getting drunk. If you ever want to get drunk, tell me and I'll buy as much as you want and you can sit here at the kitchen table and drink all night by yourself. Deal?"

It might have been a mind game, I don't know. But it worked. I never went out drinking with my friends. I never got high. And I never asked my Dad to buy me booze so I could get drunk at home.

But now, things were different. I was a few years out of high school and working with teenagers for a living. How many times had I told them not to use drugs? Saying "no" was such an easy message to preach to them because I'd never really been tempted to say "yes." People knew I wasn't into that stuff so they didn't offer me any.

Did I want some?

When those two hikers offered me some pot that day in the woods, I started thinking, *Maybe I should go ahead and try it, just this once. No one will ever know. What will it hurt to try it once? It's not like I'm gonna become an addict after a couple puffs or hurt anyone or embarrass my family or get arrested out here in the middle of nowhere. Besides, it would be good to learn what it's like so I'd know what I'm talking about when I tell teens not to do it. And hey, it's free for the taking!*

In that moment I couldn't think of any good reason *not* to accept their offer. Even though I should have known a dozen reasons, as I stood there looking at the smoking joint I forgot them all. I forgot that marijuana is the most popular illegal drug in the U.S. I forgot it can cause memory loss, hallucinations and paranoia. I forgot that it increases the risk of cancer, reduces the ability to concentrate and that it's addictive. If they'd tried to force me to take it, or pressured me to try some, I knew I would have refused. That would have been easier. But I wasn't ready for this, an innocently appearing offer, "Do you want some?"

Why not, Steve? Go ahead.

In that moment, when that guy asked me if I wanted some, I realized my answer was "yes." I did.

what are you gonna say?

You see, when you finally face that moment (and you will if you haven't already) you learn that it's not just a matter of saying "no." It's a matter of saying "no" when those voices in your head are telling you to go on, prompting you forward, pulling you in. It's a matter of saying "no" when it seems like it's okay just this one time, when it seems like nothing bad could happen, when you think no one else will ever know. Honoring the Spirit is a matter of saying "no" *when you want to say "yes."*

They stared at me waiting for a reply.

And that day, despite how easy it would have been and how tempting it was and how safe it seemed, I finally said, "Naw, I'm not into that," and continued down the trail.

I learned two things about myself that day. First, I wasn't as strong as I thought I was. None of us are immune from doing something wrong. And second, I realized how much I need to depend on God—rather than on myself—when those times of testing come. Even when no one is looking.

"If you think you are standing strong, be careful, for you, too, may fall into the same sin" (1 Corinthians 10:12).

why does God want us to be good?

A high school sophomore once asked me, "If God's grace is so great and can cover all of our faults and sins then why do we have to obey his commandments?"

In other words, "If God will forgive me anyway, why be good?" That's a good question! Scripture lists at least five specific advantages to following God and pursuing purity with our lives:

1. obedience brings blessing and freedom (john 10:10)

As I mentioned in chapter eight, God wants to give us life to the fullest. He's into pleasure, not guilt. He wants us to experience life with maximum pleasure, peace and productivity. And since he's the one who designed us, he knows best what allows us the most possible joy and freedom. And that's what he offers along the path of obedience: *I will walk about in freedom, for I have sought out your precepts"* (Psalm 119:45, NIV).

2. obedience protects you from the destructive consequences of sinful choices (james 1:13)

Sin erodes trust, disrupts relationships and engulfs us in regrets. Each time you give in to sin, it gets easier and easier to do it. Yet, every sin, no matter how innocent it might appear, has devastating and lasting consequences. AIDS. Guilt. Disease. Suffering. Addiction. Death.

Each little sin is like a snowflake on a mountaintop. Which one will cause the avalanche? No one knows. But each time the snow falls, you're one step closer to disaster. Pursuing purity is the best way to avoid the devastating consequences of sin.

3. obedience prepares you for tough times (matthew 7:24-27)

When Jesus told the story of the wise and foolish builders, he explained that the difference between the two men was that one put God's word into practice and the other didn't.

Most of the time we know what's right and what's wrong. The key is *doing* the right thing, not just *knowing* about it. Then, when the storms of life come, you'll be prepared. Obedience gives us a sturdy foundation so that we can withstand difficult times and strong temptations.

4. obedience untangles you from the chains of sin (romans 6:16)

One of my coaches used to say, "Practice makes permanent." How you practice is how you're gonna play. Once I'd learned a certain way of shooting free throws it became natural. Almost second nature. Now, years later, it would be almost impossible to learn a new way to shoot because the old shooting pattern is so engrained in my mind.

That's the way it is with sin. *"An evil man is held captive by his own sins; they are ropes that catch and hold him" (Proverbs 5:22).* Bad habits have you under their control. God wants to untangle you from the control of sinful habits.

5. obedience frees you to impact the world for Christ (matthew 5:16)

I had a friend in college named Adrian Naharim. He was the president of the student body, manager of the men's basketball team, and a confessing Christian. He went on to become the principal at a junior high school in California. A few years later, I heard he'd been arrested for sexually abusing some boys at his school. Adrian spent the next three years in prison.

What do you think happened to Adrian's witness? After he'd sexually abused those children do you think unbelievers were more interested in hearing about his God or less interested?

Moral meltdowns cause us to lose credibility in the eyes of unbelievers. Disobedience undermines God's efforts to reach the world with his love. To make Christianity attractive, we must wear (and model) the clothes we say are so fashionable. Disobedience can destroy your witness to others and cause them to disregard your claims about Jesus Christ.

you don't have to be good

Here's some surprising news: Christians don't have to obey God's commandments. We *get* to. Obedience is no longer a burden or an obligation. It's a privilege. Obedience is a response to Christ's love, not the means of obtaining it. We obey because we want our lives to bring honor to God.

The key to obedience isn't effort, but submission. Obedience has more to do with relying on God for strength than with trying harder to control ourselves. Without tapping into God, our source of strength and hope, we're like a cell phone that hasn't been recharged. Or a toaster that isn't plugged in. Or a flashlight without any batteries. We're powerless to perform like we're supposed to.

But when we depend on God for strength, answers, guidance and results, then magnificent, sweet-smelling fruit is produced: *"But when the Holy Spirit controls our lives, he will produce this kind of fruit in us: love, joy, peace, patience, kindness, goodness, faithfulness, gentleness, and self-control"* (Galatians 5:22, 23).

It's tough to fake this kind of fruit because it grows naturally from the heart.

internal obedience

Jesus always had harsh words for those who just went through the motions, but had no inner love or devotion to God. He was also tough on those who claimed to love him, but refused to obey him.

God wants people who love him so much they can't help but show it. Without the Holy Spirit, this would be impossible. But with the Holy Spirit's help and guidance, it won't even be burdensome! It'll become a natural way of life: *"This is love for God: to obey his commands. And his commands are not burdensome"* (1 John 5:3, 4, NIV).

A true follower of Christ will seek ways to honor God, rather than just please herself. And obedience honors God. If you discover you're living a sinful lifestyle and you continue to deliberately disobey God without any desire to change, you're not truly a believer. The New Testament repeats this principle over and over:

Jesus said it: *"Not all people who sound religious are really godly. They may refer to me as 'Lord,' but they still won't enter the Kingdom of Heaven. The decisive issue is whether they obey my Father in heaven"* (Matthew 7:21).

The **writer of Hebrews** said it: *"Dear friends, if we deliberately continue sinning after we have received a full knowledge of the truth, there is no other sacrifice that will cover these sins. There will be nothing to look forward to but the terrible expectation of God's judgment and the raging fire that will consume his enemies"* (Hebrews 10:26, 27).

John wrote about it: *"And how can we be sure that we belong to him? By obeying his commandments. If someone says, 'I belong to God,' but doesn't obey God's commandments, that person is a liar and does not live in the truth. But those who obey God's word really do love him. That is the way to know whether or not we live in him. Those who say they live in God would live their lives as Christ did"* (1 John 2:3-6).

It doesn't mean you'll never mess up again when you become a believer. It doesn't even mean you'll always *want* to do the right thing. But it does mean that your life will be marked by a desire to honor God. And you'll naturally look for ways to serve and obey God rather than excuses not to. Obedience is how believers show their love for God.

obedience is more than being good

Just being good doesn't necessarily please God. Faith has to be at the heart of your actions and lifestyle. If you've been avoiding certain things because you're afraid of getting in trouble for doing them, set your sights higher. You've been aiming too low with your life: *"So our aim is to please him always" (2 Corinthians 5:9).*

The more you discover God's will and seek to follow it, the more your faith will change the way you live. The secret to living a life in agreement with your beliefs lies in pursuing God, and then letting him change you. *"Every child of God defeats this evil world by trusting Christ to give the victory" (1 John 5:4).*

Are you looking for a practical way to express your love for God? Then begin learning and obeying his commands. God doesn't want us to serve him out of obligation or guilt, but in freedom expressed through love. True obedience always starts in the heart!

when faced with tough moral choices, ask yourself:

Would I do this if . . .
- I knew it was going to appear in the headlines tomorrow?
- I knew it would be the last thing I ever did?
- Jesus were standing right beside me watching me do it?

For a helpful guide on how to act when faced with tough choices, check out Psalm 101. In this Psalm, David promises to live a life of integrity by pursuing purity in what he does (verse 2), what he looks at (verse 3), what he thinks about (verse 4) and the people he hangs out with (verses 5-8). Follow his example in your life today!

spiritual incense twenty
we honor the Spirit when we stop making excuses and humbly obey God's word

Obeying God means disobeying yourself. Jesus came to do his Father's will rather than whatever he wanted to do (John 6:38). Both the desire and the ability to obey come from God.

"Put into action God's saving work in your lives, obeying God with deep reverence and fear. For God is working in you, giving you the desire to obey him and the power to do what pleases him" *(Philippians 2:12, 13).*

God doesn't want us to be good to try and earn his favor; it's a practical way of showing our love for him. Obedience puts us on the right track to receive all the best that life has to offer. Obedience protects us from the consequences of destructive choices, frees us from guilt and regrets and releases us to impact the world for Christ.

So why be good? It boils down to this: It honors the God who loves you. And that's reason enough.

"Your decrees are wonderful. No wonder I obey them!" *(Psalm 119:129).*

what if i could have done more?

Why is it important to share my faith? What if I don't really know what to say? What if I'm scared of what others might think of me?

A refreshing breeze brushed against my cheek. I peered through my sunglasses across Phantom Lake.

"Hey, Steve, your shift is over. Take a break," Mike called from the deck below my feet. Mike and I were both counselors at Camp Phantom Lake. I slid off the lifeguarding chair and he ascended.

I took off my whistle and hung it on the board behind me. "Thanks. See you in a bit, I'm gonna hop in myself. It sure is hot today."

Some of the guys from my cabin were swimming in the shallow water so I began to splash around with them, letting them chase me. I dove underwater and spun around.

Tweet! Tweet!

"Buddy check! Everyone quiet!" Mike yelled.

Everyone stopped swimming and waited for the lifeguards to count the groups.

Tweet!

"Okay, swim!"

The whistle blast meant everyone was accounted for. If even one person had been missing we would've started searching for a body along the cloudy, weed-infested lake bottom. We practiced simulated emergency drills each week, but we'd never had to do it for real.

I let my boys chase me for a few minutes and then I challenged them, "See if you guys can get me under!"

"Okay!" they shouted.

First they tried the frontal attack. But they were all third and fourth grade kids and I was twice their size. One by one I picked them up and flipped them back into the water. I felt like Godzilla.

Then they tried regrouping and attacking me from all sides at once. I spun around, laughed, ducked under the water and swam about 15 feet. I resurfaced near the dock at the edge of the swimming area.

But instead of hearing the cheers or shouts of the guys, I heard screams and whistle blasts. Everyone was rushing toward shore.

"he's not breathing!"

"Clear the water! Emergency! Emergency!"

I looked around.

Ten feet away from me Mike was supporting a body. But it didn't look real. The boy's face was swollen and bluish-purple. His open eyes looked like pale marbles staring at the blazing sun. His skin looked waxy and gray. He'd been under for awhile.

Now, another lifeguard named Allison was at Mike's side walking the body toward the dock.

It's a drill, I thought. *It's a waterfront emergency drill and they're using a dummy. Some kind of mannequin. How could anyone drown in the shallow area?*

But as I climbed the ladder to the dock, I could tell this was no drill. I recognized the boy's face. I'd seen him swimming with me a few minutes earlier.

They heaved him onto the dock.

"Somebody call 911! Notify the office! Sound the emergency siren! And get these campers out of here!"

I rushed to evacuate the campers from the beach. Everyone was shouting and confused. One of the lifeguards was running up to the office to call an ambulance. Another was leaning over the boy's body, beginning rescue breathing. It wasn't like in the drills when we sort of joked around and just pretended. This wasn't pretend.

"Who knows CPR?" someone asked. At that time in Wisconsin, lifeguards weren't required to be trained in CPR. I'd taken a course the year before, but suddenly I felt like I couldn't remember anything.

"Who knows CPR?"

One of the head lifeguards is on her way. She's running down the hill. She'll be here in just a few moments. She'll know what to do.

"Does anyone here know CPR?" Mike yelled.

No, what if I did something wrong? What if I forgot an important step! Wait for Liz. Wait for Liz.

"Is he breathing? Does he have a pulse?"

There were so many things happening all at once it was hard to know who was speaking to whom.

"This kid isn't breathing!"

But, here was Liz! And she was starting CPR. And now the kid seemed to be responding. He spit up water and vomit and they turned him on his side. Good. That was good, right? But he still wasn't moving.

"Does he have a pulse?"

Liz was leaning over him. It was hard to see what was happening. A towel? You need a towel? Here. I handed them my towel. Now I could hear the sirens whining through camp. It was almost over. Almost over. The kid was shaking and coughing and shivering. Having convulsions.

All at once, the ambulance arrived and they took him away.

And suddenly we were standing there on an empty beach, breathlessly watching the ambulance rumble down the dirt road that led to the camp's entrance. And the day didn't seem so hot anymore. It felt chilly and as cold as death.

could i have done more?

The camp director called all the lifeguards to his office soon afterward. "Tell me what happened out there this morning."

Mike talked through the events surrounding the drowning, aided every once in a while by Allison. I didn't say much of anything. Liz explained that the boy hadn't been breathing, but that she'd found a pulse.

"Steve, were you there, too?" The camp director turned to me. For a moment I was silent and then everyone was staring at me.

"Yeah, I was swimming. I . . . um . . . wasn't on duty. And then when they pulled him out I helped herd the campers up the hill to clear the swimming area. I gave them my towel—"

"Okay, well, I want everyone to write up a report of what happened and turn it in to me as soon as possible. That's all for now. You can go back to your cabins."

"What about the boy?" Allison asked. "Is he gonna be okay?"

"We don't know yet," the camp director responded grimly. "The hospital hasn't told us either way."

No one said anything to me about not doing CPR. We'd all followed procedures the best we knew. Right? So why did I feel so guilty? Why was I blaming myself for this kid not breathing? I hadn't been on duty. I wasn't the one responsible. There was no way I should have been expected to see him go under.

Yet, one horrifying thought flickered in my mind . . . *what if I could have done more?*

I'd never taken lifeguarding seriously. And when the chips were down, I didn't step up to do CPR. I'd never really thought of learning CPR as a matter of life and death. And I'd just thought of lifeguarding as a cool way to catch the rays.

And now someone might be dead.

What if this kid dies and I could have done something to save him?

Later that day we heard the boy had a condition called epilepsy which causes people to have seizures during which they black out, lose muscle control or become unconscious. After examining him, his doctor verified that he'd experienced one of these seizures underwater. He'd ducked underwater while playing with his friends and had never come up. It must have happened right after the buddy check.

Finally, word came from the hospital. He'd started breathing again and they were able to clear his lungs of fluid. The kid was gonna be all right. He even returned to camp at the end of the week. Nobody was blamed. It wasn't anyone's fault. Our procedures were improved, and we all learned something. But that's not quite the end of the story.

A lot of us changed the way we looked at lifeguarding after that. We began to take it very seriously. We finally understood the life and death importance of what we'd been asked to do.

pulled from the depths

A few years later I was lifeguarding at another camp when a 13-year-old boy jumped off the end of the pier and began to flail his arms and beat the water. At first he looked like he was just messing around, but then he began to sink beneath the surface. This time I didn't hesitate. I ran into the water to pull him out. Another student was nearby, and together we grabbed for the drowning boy. I'll never forget seeing his face as he sank back away from me through the murky water, reaching for my hand.

If our hands hadn't met, he might never have come up. After I helped him out of the water he thanked me. Boy, did he thank me!

I'm sure he didn't care how many classes I'd attended, lifeguarding books I'd read or whether or not I had a little certification card on file in the office. He was thankful because I'd put into practice what I knew, and saved his life.

Lifeguarding isn't the only important thing people don't always take seriously. Sometimes we treat our faith in God the same way. We go to church and hear about how important it is to share Christ's love, but too often we make excuses for doing nothing. Or, we just go through the motions. We don't usually consider sharing our faith with others a matter of life and death.

"It's the pastor's job to tell people about Jesus. That's what he gets paid for."
"What if they ask me a question I don't know? I'd look stupid."
"I'll wait for the right opportunity. There's no hurry."

Yet a main part of the job description of being a Christian is rescuing other people. People drifting away from God. People who are spiritually drowning.

what's the point?

"For God was in Christ, reconciling the world to himself, no longer counting people's sins against them. This is the wonderful message he has given us to tell others" (2 Corinthians 5:19).

You wanna have beautiful feet? Tell someone good news, *"How beautiful are the feet of those who bring good news!" (Romans 10:15).* You wanna have *incredibly* beautiful feet? Tell someone the best news of all.

When Jesus returns, the last thing you want to be doing is standing there, wondering if you could have done more to save someone.

Saving someone's life is something you'll never regret. Sharing with him or her the new life Jesus offers is even better. Because it lasts forever.

> *"But thanks be to God, who made us his captives and leads us along in Christ's triumphal procession. Now wherever we go he uses us to tell others about the Lord and to spread the Good News like a sweet perfume" (2 Corinthians 2:14).*

Long ago when a king won a war, he led the enemy captives in a victory parade through his capital. The people threw roses and flowers on everyone to celebrate the victory. And everyone left smelling like the conquering king.

In these verses, Paul compares believers to God's captives. The war against sin, Satan and death is over. God dethroned the devil and took back his kingdom. God won! All of us who used to be God's enemies have been brought into the city of God for a party. Now we're free to go into the world to spread the news. And the fragrance lingers in our lives. Everywhere we go to tell people that the war is over, we smell like the celebration and the conquering King. We smell like God!

investing in eternity

When Jesus returned to Heaven he left the responsibility of sharing the Good News of God's love with his followers. It's our job to share it. Not out of guilt. Not out of obligation. But because of love for Jesus and a desire to see people set free from sin's destruction. It's at the heart of following Jesus and smelling like God.

We don't rely on our own strength or cleverness. That's not the way to accomplish great things for God. We rely on God's Spirit working through us to change lives.

> *"It is not that we think we can do anything of lasting value by ourselves. Our only power and success come from God" (2 Corinthians 3:5).*

The New Testament book of Mark tells the story of Jesus' life. And in the entire book, the only people Jesus ever got angry with were those who got in the way of other people trying to find God. God wants you to bring others to him. Not force them. Not coerce them. Just boldly share his message with them.

And then stand back in awe as God performs spiritual CPR.

spiritual incense twenty-one
we honor the Spirit when we share the good news of salvation with others

If you found an awesome new website, discovered a cool store at the mall or rented a hilarious movie, you'd recommend it to your friends. That's all God asks of you. Recommend him to your friends.

Stick to the truth, stay on track, keep it simple and avoid arguments. You don't have to know everything. If someone asks you something you don't know, look it up, then get back to the person!

Your job is to share the message, God's job is to work in the heart of your friend. Stick to doing your job and let God do his.

When you share the good news with others, not only will you have beautiful feet, the rest of you will smell pretty nice as well!

It has been said, "God doesn't call you to be successful, just faithful."

when you share the gospel with someone, remember to clearly explain that:

- God loves you and wants a relationship with you (John 3:16).
- Your personal sin has harmed your intimacy with God. Sin results in physical death and spiritual separation from God (Romans 6:23).
- Jesus Christ lived a perfect life to fulfill God's requirements and he died to make us right with God. He is the only solution for our sin problem (1 John 2:2).

- When we trust Jesus as our Savior from sin, we receive God's forgiveness and become members of his family (1 John 1:8, 9).
- Heaven is God's gift to us. We can never be good enough to earn it, only receive it by faith (Ephesians 2:8, 9).
- If we reject God's offer of salvation, we will be punished forever (Matthew 25:46).

to review, there are seven spiritual truths that will help you smell like God. we honor the Holy Spirit when we . . .

- Number one: Seek his will and pursue our relationship with God.
- Number two: Prayerfully let God guide us in the choices we make every day.
- Number three: Make the most of each day and value heavenly things above earthly ones.
- Number four: Continue to trust in God even when life doesn't make sense.
- Number five: Pursue purity in our thoughts, words and actions.
- Number six: Stop making excuses and humbly obey God's Word.
- Number seven: Share the Good News of salvation with others.

God, sometimes I'm scared of what other people think. I'm scared of what might happen if I start telling them about you. But you are the only hope for a dying world! Help me to put into practice the truths that I know and reach out to others to rescue them. I want to live like Jesus. I want to smell like you. Amen.

i thought i smelled something!

God sent Jesus to suffer in your place and pay the penalty for your sins. Trusting in Christ as your Savior is the only way to have a right relationship with God. Before you can start to smell like God, you need to get to know and believe in the one true God.

Then, follow Jesus and let him change you from the inside out. Following God isn't based on a set of rules, but on deepening your relationship with him and letting him rule in your life.

Finally, let the Holy Spirit guide you into a life of purity that spreads the fragrance of Heaven throughout your world. And as you go, God goes with you. To touch the lives of others with the aroma of his love. Out of gratitude for what God has done, you can honor him by taking the message of his love to the world.

To know him. To serve him. To honor him. That's what it means to smell like God.

Serving God is the ultimate adventure and Heaven is the ultimate destination. May your life burn with its supernatural scent! I pray that I'll see you (and smell you) there, someday soon!

If you became a believer in Jesus Christ through reading this book, I'd love to hear from you! Please contact me at:

NextGen Ministries
P.O. Box 141
Johnson City, TN 37605-0141
www.nextgenministries.com

Blessings!
Steven James

appendix

[1]paul's description of God:

a. "He is the God who made the world and everything in it.

b. Since he is Lord of heaven and earth, he doesn't live in man-made temples, and human hands can't serve his needs—for he has no needs.

c. He himself gives life and breath to everything, and he satisfies every need there is.

d. From one man he created all the nations throughout the whole earth. He decided beforehand which should rise and fall, and he determined their boundaries.

e. His purpose in all of this was that the nations should seek after God and perhaps feel their way toward him and find him—though he is not far from any one of us.

f. For in him we live and move and exist. As one of your own poets says, 'We are his offspring.'

g. And since this is true, we shouldn't think of God as an idol designed by craftsmen from gold or silver or stone.

h. God overlooked people's former ignorance about these things, but now he commands everyone everywhere to turn away from idols and turn to him.

i. For he has set a day for judging the world with justice by the man he has appointed, and he proved to everyone who this is by raising him from the dead."

j. When they heard Paul speak of the resurrection of a person who had been dead, some laughed, but others said, 'We want to hear more about this later.' That ended Paul's discussion with them, but some joined him and became believers. Among them were Dionysius, a member of the Council, a woman named Damaris, and others." (Acts 17:24-34)

what that means to us today:

a. There is only one God. He is all-powerful. He planned and created the universe.

b. He is ruler of all that there is both physically and spiritually. God is self-existent and doesn't live in a physical realm. You can't contain him. Rather, God exists everywhere at once.

c. God is the source of all life. He provides for our needs day by day.

d. God created human life. Your ancestors didn't evolve from a monkey or climb from the slime. All the events in history are in God's hands. He controls them and nothing takes him by surprise. Nothing happens by chance in the universe. God is in control.

e. There is purpose to the universe. God's plan all along has been for human beings to seek him. That was his purpose in creation, civilization and history. God is within the reach of every heart.

f. We depend on God to preserve our lives, to give us existence and meaning.

g. We shouldn't pretend that we can create our own "god" the way we want. We don't tell God the way it is—he tells us!

h. Now that Christ has come, God holds everyone accountable for his or her life, choices, and sins. God commands people to turn from their sins and turn to him. Whatever you desire more than God is an idol to you.

i. One day Jesus will return to judge people. And God is fair, he doesn't grade on a curve. Those who have turned to him will be pardoned. Those who have not, will be sentenced. The proof of God's plan was Jesus' resurrection.

j. People respond differently when they hear about the resurrection. Some laugh. Some put off making a commitment to Christ. And some become believers. Which one will you be?

endnotes

[2]John 11:25, 26

[3]John 3:17, 18

[4]John 3:36

[5]Romans 6:23

[6]Jesus refers to Judas going to Hell in John 17:12. Peter refers to it in Acts 1:25.

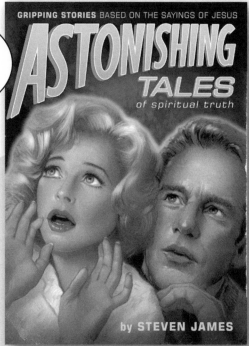